SELF-EST
THE KEY TO YOUR (

Over 160,000 copies of Tony Humphreys' books have already sold in the English language. Currently there are twenty-three foreign translations.

Books by Tony Humphreys
All About Children
A Different Kind of Teacher
The Power of 'Negative' Thinking
Myself, My Partner
A Different Kind of Discipline
Work and Worth: Take Back Your Life
Whose Life Are You Living?
Leaving the Nest: What Families Are All About

Audio-tapes and CDs by Tony Humphreys
Self-Esteem for Adults
Raising Your Child's Self-esteem
Work and Self

SELF–ESTEEM
THE KEY TO YOUR CHILD'S FUTURE

Tony Humphreys

BA, HDE, MA, PhD

Newleaf

Newleaf

an imprint of

Gill & Macmillan Ltd

Hume Avenue, Park West, Dublin 12

with associated companies throughout the world

www.gillmacmillan.ie

ISBN-13: 978 07171 3790 9
ISBN-10: 0 7171 3790 2

Index compiled by Helen Litton
Print origination by Carrigboy Typesetting Services, Co. Cork
Printed in Malaysia

*The paper used in this book comes from the wood pulp of managed
forests. For every tree felled, at least one tree is planted, thereby
renewing natural resources.*

This book is typeset in 10pt on 14pt AfgarRotisSemisans.

A CIP catalogue record for this book is available from the British Library.

5 4 3 2

To the memory of my parents

CONTENTS

INTRODUCTION

The self-esteem of children is central to their educational development. Mounting research evidence, as well as the experience of school
teachers, remedial teachers, family therapists, clinical psychologists,
counsellors and educational psychologists, indicates that most
children who are troubled and have learning difficulties within
classrooms come from problematic home situations and have self-
esteem difficulties. The resolution of conflicts within homes and the
elevation of children's self-esteem are major responsibilities for
parents and determine not only their children's educational development but also their emotional, social and sexual development.

By the time children come to school their self-esteem has been
largely forged. Certainly, teachers can add to or detract from
children's self-esteem, but the sources of children's self-esteem
problems lie primarily within the home. Each parent's own level of
self-esteem influences that of the child. Parents with high self-
esteem effect high self-esteem in their children but, sadly, the
converse is also true. Another source of children's insecurities is
how their parents relate to each other. Particularly in their early
years, children are totally dependent on parents and when parents
are in conflict with each other the children's security is greatly
threatened. It is little wonder that children coming from troubled
homes find it difficult to apply themselves to school work. Too
often these children will receive a critical and sometimes even a

harsh response from teachers, thereby confirming their worst fears that this world is not a safe and secure place in which to be.

Children's educational development is also affected by how their parents relate to them and whether the parents know how to develop children's self-esteem. Furthermore, parents are the children's first educators and knowledge of what to teach and how to teach are important skills. Parents need to know about the behavioural management of children; they need to understand the nature and purpose of children's problematic behaviours and how to respond constructively to them.

Parenting is the hardest job of all: it is not a 'natural' ability but a complex and multifaceted one for which little or no training is given. If parents are to prepare their children for the challenges of school they need to focus on the following areas:

- the couple relationship
- the nature of the love shown to children
- resolution of family conflicts
- how they feel about themselves
- the mirroring of the self-worth of each child
- helping the child who is troubled
- parents as educators.

This book then focuses on these topics. Parental effectiveness relies on each parent's sense of their own worth (Chapter 5), on how they relate to each other (Chapter 2) and on what kind of loving environment they both set out to create (Chapter 3). Effectiveness is also enhanced when parents know how to resolve conflicts when they arise and when they possess good behavioural management skills in relation to both themselves and their children (Chapter 4). The mirroring of the self-worth of each child is a complex process, and knowledge of the nature of self-worth and self-esteem and how self-worth can be effectively mirrored is also essential (Chapter 6). Children manifest a variety of emotional, behavioural and social problems; an understanding of these problems and the development of constructive ways of responding to them will lead to the maintenance, and often the further realisation, of a child's self-worth (Chapter 7). Finally, this book explores the role of parents as educators and sets out guidelines on how parents can foster their children's natural curiosity to learn so that during their school life a love of learning will continue to grow (Chapter 8).

The book provides the reader with relevant case studies and offers tried and tested ways of achieving the aims set out above. At the end of each chapter there is a summary of the important insights and the key actions that will bring about the changes needed to resolve children's emotional and educational problems. Each chapter of the book stands on its own and individual sections of a chapter can be consulted to understand and resolve some particular difficulty that may have arisen in a child's, parent's or couple's life. To begin with, it is a good idea to read the book through in order to get an overall sense of my ways of understanding and resolving children's emotional, social and educational problems.

The book is aimed particularly at parents of school-going children, but it has relevance for anybody interested in the emotional, social and educational development of children. It has particular relevance for teachers who can use it to work together with parents who are the primary educators of their children and who can be an essential support and back-up. It offers insights into why children may come to school being emotionally vulnerable and having poor self-esteem, and shows how these problems can be resolved. The book may be of value to home–school liaison officers, to students in teacher training and to community workers, social workers, psychologists and counsellors involved with children who are distressed. It could also be used by groups of parents to work through together some of the issues involved in effective parenting.

The book is a product of my own life experiences, my work as a primary and secondary teacher, my professional involvement with teachers at both staff and individual levels and, most of all, my work as a clinical psychologist helping families, couples, individual adults, adolescents and children who are deeply troubled. In my experience parents are always eager to provide the best for their children but sometimes they are not aware of the blocks to attaining this aspiration and of how to overcome them. My hope is that this book will assist parents in overcoming such blocks.

Finally, the case studies described in the book have been sufficiently masked to ensure anonymity.

CHAPTER 1

SELF-ESTEEM AND YOUR CHILD'S EDUCATION

SELF-ESTEEM AND THE SCHOOL-GOING CHILD

A child enters a classroom carrying within her the effects of relationships with significant adults in her life. The most crucial relationship is the one with parents. A child will also be affected by experiences with grandparents (particularly when they live under the same roof), aunts, uncles and child-minders. These relationships are the looking glass through which the child develops her self-esteem. By the time she comes to school, a child has already established an image of herself and that image may be further affected by her experiences with teachers and peers.

It is now known that children who have learning difficulties in school frequently have self-esteem problems, and what is most needed is an affirmation of their self-worth before effective academic development can be established. Teachers can do much to help children feel good about themselves but the involvement of parents is crucial as most of all the child needs to be loved and accepted by her parents and to impress them. However, if the school-going child has a highly protective self-esteem it is likely that the parents (biological, foster or adoptive) also have self-esteem protectors. Parents and teachers who possess a good sense of themselves are in a position to help children feel good about themselves but the converse is also true. This process happens whether or not the parents and the other significant adults in the child's life realise it. Every action, facial expression, gesture and verbal interaction on the part of significant adults in the child's life communicates some message to the child about her worth, value and capability.

NATURE OF SELF-WORTH AND SELF-ESTEEM

There tends to be confusion in understanding the concepts of self-worth and self-esteem, often leading to misguided helping.

Self-worth is a given, unchangeable; it is what you are from the moment of conception: sacred, worthy of giving and receiving love, unique, individual, possessing vast intellectual potential and giftedness. Self-worth cannot be damaged or taken from you, it is always there; but for many people it lies hidden behind defensive walls. Your self-worth has to do with your unique being and no behaviour either adds or takes from your person. It is when the person of a child or adult begins to be seen through her behaviour that self-esteem emerges as a protection against not being loved and valued for self.

Self-esteem is a screen self, a crust you form around your real self in order to survive either in the social system of which you are a member or in particular relationships. The greater the threats to your expression of your self-worth, the lower is your self-esteem and the higher are your protectors. Basically, self-esteem is the amount of your real self that you dare show to people. It is in this sense that self-esteem is a screen, because it hides or veils what would be threatening to reveal. For example, each child is unique, individual and different. However, difference has not been affirmed and celebrated in Irish culture, where children (and adults) conform to the demand to be the same in homes, classrooms, churches, communities and sports fields. The word con-form illustrates powerfully how self-esteem is developed as a shadow, a veil over what would be threatening to show – difference. 'Con' means 'false' and 'form' means 'image'. To conform makes you create a false image, a shadow self that hides the aspect(s) of real self that is not accepted.

The more characteristics of your true self that are not affirmed, or, on appearance, are severely punished and violated, the greater the defensive screen created by the person. There are individuals who describe themselves, for example, as 'stupid', 'evil', 'vile', 'ugly', 'unlovable', 'hateful', 'bad'. These persons created these self-esteem defences as a means of survival and, not surprisingly, it takes considerable patience on the part of others to help them to let go of their shadow selves.

There is a certain joy and comfort in being hidden, as it reduces further exposure to rejection and neglect; but what a disaster not to come to a place of being able fully to express your sacred, unique and amazing presence.

There is an inverse relationship between your level of self-esteem and your level of protectors. For instance, if your early experiences were of a loveless and harsh nature, you would emerge from childhood with low self-esteem and with remarkably high protectors. The person with low self-esteem may either be very aggressive, violent, blaming, workaholic, alcohol dependent and possessive, or be extremely passive, withdrawn, apathetic, drug-addicted, shy, timid, fearful and depressed.

Many people fall into the area of having middle self-esteem where they hide only some aspects of their true selves and where their defensive manoeuvres are moderate in nature. A person with middle self-esteem may describe himself as, 'I'm not all bad', 'I'm your average man', 'I'm as good as the next person', 'There are people worse than me'. Their protectors would be either being argumentative, inflexible, over-ambitious and hypersensitive to criticism, or being dependent, fearful, anxious, uncertain, tentative and concerned about how others see them. Nevertheless, this group are much closer to their self-worth than those with low self-esteem.

People with high self-esteem, which accounts for about 5-10 per cent of the population, are very close to the full expression of their unique presence and worth, but because we live in a world where the threats to being truly yourself are frequent, intense and enduring, some small level of protection is required. Nevertheless, persons with high self-esteem are those who work out mostly from their immutable self-worth and hence are loving, capable of receiving love, spontaneous, unique, different, individual, expansive, adventurous, creative and fearless.

It is important to understand that self-esteem arises in response to threats to the true expression of self and is an amazing and creative defence by those children and adults whose self-worth is threatened. Change can only begin with the acceptance of the shadow self as being a necessary 'evil'; such embracing of your present level of self-esteem is the first step on the journey back to your real self. Stanislavsky, the Russian dramatist and thinker, wrote: 'The longest and most exciting journey is the journey inwards.'

There are two central dimensions to self-esteem: *the feeling of being lovable* and the *feeling of being capable*. Is your school-going child shy, timid, overly reserved, extremely quiet, attention-seeking and clinging or is she aggressive and bullying? If so, these are indications that the child doubts her lovability. Is your child frightened of and resistant to new challenges, fearful of failure, easily upset by mistakes, nervous of school tests, perfectionist, overly diligent about school work or evasive of homework? If so, these are indicators of the child's doubts about her capability.

Examples of behaviour that show a child has poor to middle self-esteem are given below. These behaviours are signs of the inner turmoil of children and positive responses are needed when they are shown. It is useful to categorise these signs as *overcontrol* and *undercontrol* indicators. Children manifesting undercontrol of behaviour are more likely to be brought for psychological help, because their problematic behaviours can seriously interfere with the functioning of parents or teachers or both. The child who shows overcontrol of behaviour is often more at risk but this can be missed by parents and others as the child's symptoms do not upset adults' lives.

SELF-ESTEEM AND CHILDREN'S LEARNING DIFFICULTIES

The way parents respond to the self-esteem protectors of their children will be determined largely by their own levels of self-esteem. When parents themselves have doubts about their own value and capability they tend to be either overdemanding or overprotective, or may even be neglectful, of their children. This results in the children also developing self-esteem protectors. For example, the children of teachers are more at risk than any other professional group, because teachers tend to demand high academic performance from their children and tend to scold, ridicule, criticise and condemn failure. All children want to please their parents and the possibility of humiliation through criticism and the withdrawal of love will lead to two possible reactions in children. One reaction is apathy and avoidance. Here the child withdraws from making

CHECKLIST FOR LOW (HIGHLY PROTECTIVE) SELF-ESTEEM IN SCHOOL-GOING CHILDREN

Overcontrol protectors

- ☐ Shy and withdrawn
- ☐ Unusually quiet
- ☐ Reluctant to take on new activities/challenges
- ☐ Clinging to one or both parents
- ☐ Having difficulties in mixing with other children
- ☐ Overly conscientious or apathetic in learning situations
- ☐ Fearful and timid in new situations
- ☐ Easily upset when positively corrected
- ☐ Extremely upset when negatively corrected
- ☐ Inclined to day-dream
- ☐ Fearful of mistakes and failures
- ☐ In the habit of putting self down
- ☐ Always trying to please people
- ☐ Complaining of abdominal pain and nausea

Undercontrol protectors

- ☐ Aggressive
- ☐ Having regular temper tantrums
- ☐ Boastful
- ☐ Regularly playing truant from school
- ☐ Uncooperative when requested to do things
- ☐ Frequently requesting help or reassurance
- ☐ Continually asking if she is loved or wanted
- ☐ Avoiding school lessons though risking parents' disapproval
- ☐ Blaming of others for own mistakes
- ☐ Destructive of own or others' belongings
- ☐ Careless when carrying out home or school assignments

academic and other efforts because to try means risking humiliation and rejection. The child subconsciously reasons: 'with no effort, no failure; with no failure, no humiliation'. What an immensely clever strategy! But, such children are often labelled as 'lazy', 'dull', 'stupid' or 'useless'. Without attention to their self-worth these children will not progress academically.

The second reaction of children when their self-worth is threatened is compensation. This is evident in the child who is intense, who is a perfectionist, who spends too many hours over school work or who is easily upset by any prospect of failure. Again, the wisdom of the strategy is commendable. By working so hard the child is attempting to eliminate any prospect of failure as failure and mistakes mean risking the disapproval of parents and teachers. This child misses out in other aspects of a child's life such as play, friendships, sports activities and enjoyment of learning. For this child identity is tied to behaviour – particularly academic behaviour – and unless this identity issue is resolved the child will become even more chronically insecure, perfectionist and hard-working as the academic pressures continue to increase during school life.

Another type of compensation is seen in the child who is boastful, aggressive or bullying and who acts in a superior way. However, she rarely makes any effort and any pressure from others to academically apply herself results in a protective response such as: 'I could do it if I wanted to but why should I please you?' Like the child who either uses the avoidance strategy or overworks, the child displaying such arrogance is really protecting herself against any possibility of failure, as, once again, failure would mean humiliation and rejection.

Many adults also use these strategies of avoidance and compensation. For example, the most common phobia of all is that of public speaking. Ninety per cent of people avoid such an undertaking. Such avoidance is a clear indicator of doubts about capability and ability to impress others. Likewise, many parents put high demands and expectations on themselves in order to avoid any prospect of mistakes and failure. Many parents say that they have not put verbal pressure on their children to succeed academically. This may be the case but actions speak much louder than words and it is the parents' lifestyle that mainly affects children. Children protectively believe that their parents are always right and as a result they imitate their actions indiscriminately and become like them. In adolescence children think parents know nothing. But this attitude is relatively short-lived as the dependence on parents is far stronger than this transitory rebellion. Some children will develop a pattern of behaviour that is diametrically opposed to that of their parents – but which is equally extreme and results in an unhappy and problematic life. For example, the child who drops out of school in reaction to pressure for academic performance from parents builds up a whole new series of problems for herself.

It has been shown that parents who put pressure on the child for academic performance unwittingly blind themselves to the child's self-worth and this leads to either avoidance or compensation by the child to prevent further hurt. But what about the parent who over-protects and puts little or no pressure on children to make responsible efforts? If the overly demanding parent causes children to become insecure and lacking in confidence, the overly protective parent brings about similar vulnerabilities in his child. The parent who does everything for the child and does not make reasonable demands on her communicates no message of belief in the child's wondrous capacity to learn and to become independent. Protection disables children and keeps them dependent and helpless. These children may feel loved but they will in no way feel capable.

SELF-ESTEEM AND THE CHILD'S MOTIVATION TO LEARN

Parents are often puzzled by children who clearly possess the skills but make no effort to learn. The child with high self-esteem retains a natural curiosity for learning and is enthusiastic when presented with a new challenge. This child is confident in social situations and in tackling academic challenges. On the other hand, the child with middle to low self-esteem has lost the excitement of learning; any learning means risking failure and mistakes and these have only brought about humiliation and rejection in the past. It is safer to risk a parent's or teacher's disapproval than the embarrassment and punishment of failure.

Success and failure in themselves have no effect on a child's motivation to learn but the reactions of parents, teachers and other significant adults to success and failure can have a devastating effect. When adults react positively to successful performance and punishingly to failure (for example shouting, blaming, scolding, comparing), the child begins to doubt her ability to live up to expectations. Many parents (and teachers) have difficulty in understanding that praising the successful performance of an activity breeds dependence and consequent fears of not pleasing in children. Parents need to encourage children in their efforts to master an activity. What counts is the effort not the performance. Emphasis on performance may eventually dry up effort or lead to overtrying. Every effort on a child's part is an attainment. Think of the child who manages for the first time to put on her shoes: she presents herself to her father and says, 'hey Dad, look', proudly pointing down at her shoes. Dad looks down and responds crossly, 'you put them on the wrong feet'. The child will now feel put down, hurt and rejected. The father has totally missed that this effort is a major attainment: for the first time the child has managed to put her own shoes on her own feet. By showing that he was impressed by her effort, the father could have encouraged and guided the child to learn the next stages of shoe fitting. With the punishing reaction she is unlikely to try again or may get anxious and perfectionist on the next attempt. Without realising it, her father has undermined her self-worth. He has not yet learned that children are always lovable whether they fail or make mistakes and that they are capable of learning any skill. If a child experiences such punishing parental reactions only now and again then no serious block to self-worth occurs. However, if such reactions are a regular feature in a child's life then children develop self-esteem protectors.

An important rule for parents to be aware of is that while unrealistic demands lead to low (highly protective) self-esteem, equally no demands at all lead to low self-esteem. In both cases children are doomed to low academic achievement or overachievement. The wise parent knows that there is an optimum pressure – just enough to cause children to feel challenged and positive but not so much that they become distressed. The secret is to be aware of the child's present level of functioning and to work from there in a realistic manner.

Another important guide for parents is not to allow a child slide out of responsibility. Loving children means encouraging them and being positively firm with them in pursuing the responsible behaviours that will gain them the skills and abilities to have an independent, fulfilling and challenging life. Parents cease to love their children when they allow them to slide out of responsibility. But the challenges that are set need to be close to their present level of functioning. If the gap between their present knowledge and skill levels and what the parent is expecting of them is too wide, children will become anxious and threatened and will resort to either avoidance or compensation.

It is now well established that without attention to self-worth children are not likely to make long-term scholastic progress. Research is showing that, in general, people's levels of achievement are influenced by how they see themselves and, more specifically, that self-esteem and academic achievement are strongly associated. Parents are in the most powerful position to influence how their children feel about themselves. The most important medium of influence parents have is their relationship with their children and when this is valuing and caring in nature the children's self-esteem will be elevated.

ORIGINS OF CHILDREN'S SELF-ESTEEM AND LEARNING DIFFICULTIES

Two-parent families

The self-esteem of the child is also affected by the parents' relationship with each other. The child who regularly witnesses openly hostile conflict or silent hostility between parents can become chronically insecure. Children are so dependent on parents that any threat to the couple relationship undermines their confidence that their needs will be met. Children do not understand that the conflict between their parents does not mean that they are not loved. But it is true that when marital conflict is ongoing it generally means that children's needs are neglected. Furthermore, conflictual relationships are typically characterised by self-esteem protectors on the part of each partner. In many ways the conflict in the relationship just adds further fuel to the fire of self-esteem difficulties in the offspring of such a partnership and to the self-esteem protectors of the parents. It is not surprising that children who come from a home troubled by parental conflict cannot attend to classroom activities. Very often they will not reveal these home problems and, consequently, teachers may misinterpret their inattentiveness, non-cooperation or aggression as impertinence, laziness or boldness. The teachers may then punish, ridicule, scold or withdraw affection from these children, thereby confirming their worst fears about being of no value and possessing no capability. In this way teachers add to the turmoil of home and, generally, because of their poor relationship with troubled children, pile up more management problems for themselves in the classroom.

A major determinant of self-esteem is the way members of the family interact with each other. Even though parents may have a reasonably good relationship with each other they may still have self-esteem protectors and these will largely determine their effectiveness as parents. Many parents live their lives through their children and consequently block the emergence of their own and their children's self-worth. Other parents may be neglectful, emotionally cold or overly protective – all of which lead to children creating a self-esteem screen.

Lone-parent families

Lone-parent families are a growing feature of Irish society. There is no evidence that a lone parent is any less effective than a married parent but the latter generally has the advantages of a supportive partner, better financial resources and back-up support systems. Lone parents, on the other hand, often have meagre financial resources, are sometimes alienated from their family of origin and have poor or no support systems. Not surprisingly, the stress and pressures experienced by lone parents can be far greater than those of their married counterparts. Lone parents deserve the social and psychological resources necessary for them to continue their own development as individuals and to become effective parents. When these are not present, difficulties can arise within the lone-parent family leading to a loss of a sense of good about self both in the children and in the parent. A caring and responsive social system can rescue such families.

Subcultural families

Not all the problems of children in schools are due to self-esteem protectors. Sometimes the cause is that children from a subculture are being educated in the schools of the main culture of the country. They may come, for instance, from the travelling community or an area of high unemployment or a strongly working-class area and may not have the same motivation or interest in academic development as their middle-class counterparts. Playing truant or dropping out is quite common among such children. There is quite a difference between children who develop a school phobia and those who are school truants. For the latter the problem normally resides in the school whereas for the child with a school phobia the problem lies in the home. The child who plays truant from school generally hates school and may be the victim of a teacher who is ridiculing, scolding or even violent. The child may also be a member of a subculture and may be having difficulties in adjusting to the demands of the different culture of the school she is attending. In contrast, the child who has a school phobia usually loves school and when she does manage to get there will be a model student. In this case the problem lies in the home and the child may, for example, stay home to 'look after' a mother who is being neglected by her husband or a parent who is overly dependent on the child. Sometimes the school-going child stays at home because of the arrival of a baby brother or sister and she dreads not getting her needs met should she go to school.

KEY INSIGHTS

- ☐ Children enter classrooms carrying with them the effects of their relationships with their parents and other significant adults in their lives.
- ☐ Parents' relationships with children are the looking glass through which children develop a sense of themselves.

- Children who have learning difficulties in school frequently have self-esteem protectors.
- Parents with high self-esteem reflect their children's unique worth but the converse is also true.
- When children have self-esteem protectors they will manifest these through either undercontrol or overcontrol behaviours.
- Avoidance and compensatory behaviours are attempts by children to avoid failure and mistakes as these experiences are associated with humiliation and rejection.
- Parents who put pressure on children for academic performance unwittingly cause children to become protective.
- Parents who are overly protective of their children undermine children's belief in themselves.
- Success and failure have no effect on children but the reactions of parents and teachers to success and failure can have devastating effects on children's motivation to learn.
- What counts is effort not performance.
- Emphasis on performance may eventually dry up effort or lead to overtrying.
- Children's levels of academic attainment are strongly influenced by how they see themselves.
- The most important medium of influence parents have is the relationship with their children and when this is valuing in nature children's self-esteem rises.
- The self-esteem of children is affected by the parents' relationship with each other.
- Many parents live their lives through their children and consequently block the realisation of their own and their children's self-worth.

CHAPTER 2

THE COUPLE RELATIONSHIP AND THE CHILD'S SELF-ESTEEM

SELF-ESTEEM AND THE COUPLE RELATIONSHIP

Individuals bring their self-esteem screens into the couple relationship and all the interactions between them are affected by their doubts, fears and insecurities. It is known that the first two years of marriage are the most difficult, giving rise to the saying 'love is blind but marriage is an eye-opener'. The stress in these early years arises because the couple are trying to adjust to each other's differences. Differences between a couple can be challenging and exciting and can be an opportunity to learn from each other. But when the self-esteem of one or both partners is low, differences become a major threat and can become the battleground on which each attempts to establish his or her identity at the expense of the other. For example, the aggressive partner will push that her needs, career, viewpoints and so on are more important than the other's; on the other hand, the passive partner sacrifices her own individuality for the sake of acceptance from the other and 'for peace sake'. The more extensive the self-esteem protectors of the partners the longer the problems and conflicts will endure.

Unfortunately, 'problems marry problems'. Individuals who are deeply insecure tend to marry or form relationships with persons of like vulnerability. It may seem on the surface that the two partners are opposites and the saying 'opposites attract' may often seem true. For example, the aggressive person tends to choose a passive partner. Other examples are exhibitionism being paired with inhibition, extroversion with introversion, people-pleasing with selfishness. There is subconscious wisdom in these choices of seeming opposites. The person who is aggressive needs to learn some of the passivity of her partner and vice versa. Likewise the person who is reserved, shy and quiet can learn much from an extrovert partner and vice versa.

I recall the following case of a man who married a person opposite to himself in behaviour. As a child, and for much of his adulthood, his identity was totally enmeshed with being the 'helper'. His mother had become an invalid when he was about seven years of age and he had taken over the caring role within the family. The reinforcement he got for this role was very great: 'What a wonderful child who can cook, shop, clean the house, look after his mother, do the laundry'. The condition for recognition became being the 'carer'. This early conditioning led him to take up professions in adulthood which are primarily of a caring nature: the priesthood, teaching and therapy. Without realising it, he was still getting his acceptance from others through taking care of them. It was quite a sad but freeing revelation to him when he discovered that all his giving over the years had been driven by a need to be accepted. The giving was a subconscious strategy to get recognition. Before (and for a long time after) he had arrived at the insight of his dependency on others for acceptance, he had tremendous difficulty in saying 'no' to the needs of others. He had a further difficulty in identifying and responding to his own needs.

A year into his marriage he found he was getting quite hostile towards his partner. Knowing that his hostility was an indication of something about himself, I asked him: 'What is it in you that is making you cross and irritable in this relationship?' and his answer was clear: 'I give and give and give but get little in return'. But his wife was not responsible for his needs and neither could she read his mind. It was his responsibility to let her know clearly what his emotional, social, sexual, occupational, domestic and other needs were. In fact, his wife was the ideal partner for him and someone from whom he had much to learn. Unlike him, and like his mother, she was an expert at identifying and getting her own needs met. She had come from a family in which she was the 'pet' and had generally been spoiled. The child who is spoiled is used to getting his needs met by others and this expectation continues into adult-hood. However, such people are not good at taking responsibility for themselves. The child who is overindulged is disabled and emerges into adulthood being heavily dependent on others to meet his needs. This man's wife had subconsciously chosen him in order to continue the pattern from her childhood of having her needs met by others. But she also had the opportunity of learning from him that other people have needs as well and that she was capable of being responsible for herself.

When they both discovered the sources of their marital difficulties and both attempted to move away from the protective patterns of behaviour learned in childhood, their relationship deepened enormously. A relationship can be a source of support, safety and encouragement for the development of each individual. The man's task was to establish an identity separate from his relationship with others, to begin to assert his own needs within the rela-tionship and to be independent of his partner. His wife's task was to establish her identity separate from him and others, to learn to recognise and to respond to the needs of others as well as of herself and to stand on her own two very capable feet. Now communication is much clearer in their relationship. Both of them have learned to recognise and own their own needs, to take responsibility for them and to express them within the relationship without expectation that they have to be met. A partner does not have to meet the other's needs. If there is an expectation that needs have to be met, then the partners are being conditional and dependent in relation to each other. Conditionality is a recipe for conflict in relationships.

If 'opposites attract' as often seems to be the case, it is equally true to say that 'birds of a feather flock together'. But the similarity is at the deeper, self-esteem level. In this case, the man and his wife were opposites in the way they got their needs in life met, but were similar in that they both showed high levels of dependency, extensive protectors and consequent low levels of self-esteem.

COUPLE CONFLICT AND PROTECTIVE REACTIONS

Not many couples are fortunate enough to understand and resolve difficulties as happened in this marriage. Because couples are not educated to understand relationships and rarely have much sense of the powerful influence of self-esteem, conflict between a couple can quickly begin to spiral after the 'honeymoon' period. Very often the alarm bells are present during the earlier stages of the relationship, but mutual dependence blinds the partners to the signals for change needed both within each individual and between the couple. Examples of such warning signals are: possessiveness, controlling behaviour, aggression, passivity, hypersensitivity to criticism, overinvolvement, frequent need for reassurance, jealousy, alcohol dependency, withdrawal from anything new or challenging, shyness, sulking, frequent irritability, dominance. More serious warning signals include: violence, tirades, suicide threats, suicide attempts, extreme possessiveness, withdrawal and silence for long periods of time, frequent emotional outbursts.

When the self-worth of one partner becomes threatened by the other's behaviour then protective reactions will be developed to prevent further hurt and rejection. Such protective reactions include: projection and introjection, distance regulators and non-separation regulators.

Projection and introjection

A major giveaway of false personas in a couple relationship is the use of the protective communication patterns of projection and introjection. Examples of projection include: attempts to dominate; controlling, pushing, shoving; blaming; criticising; being aggressive or overdemanding; being manipulative, passive or needy; being the martyr; being passive-aggressive. The partner who projects sees the other person as responsible for her needs and welfare, and when needs are not met, or when she is feeling fearful or depressed or generally not feeling well, her partner becomes the target of either aggressive or passive behaviours. Examples of aggressive projections include:

- □ Shouting ('You hate me, don't you?')
- □ Blaming ('You make me miserable.')
- □ Hitting
- □ Criticising ('What kind of a mess of a dinner is this?')
- □ Ridicule ('What would you know about anything?')
- □ Cynicism ('I wouldn't expect anything better from you.')
- □ Sarcasm ('Look what the cat brought home.')

All these messages project the hidden needs of the person onto her partner and are attempts to make the partner responsible for her needs. The person receiving these messages is not in a mature place to read between the lines and either will be busily defending himself against the 'put-down' behaviours or will be emotionally and physically withdrawing from the partner who is projecting. Possible hidden needs buried in the above messages are:

- ☐ 'I need to feel loved and wanted in my relationship with you.'
- ☐ 'When I come home and you ignore me I feel miserable and I need closeness with you.'
- ☐ I feel put down by you and I need you to listen and to value my opinions.'
- ☐ 'I don't like bacon and cabbage and I know I need to let you know my likes and dislikes.'
- ☐ 'I feel threatened when you show greater knowledge of a subject than I do and I feel embarrassed by my own lack of education.'
- ☐ 'I feel put down when you are sarcastic and I need you to express yourself more directly and positively.'
- ☐ 'I'm not sure what to do when you are moody and I often feel responsible for your change in moods.'

Many passive-manipulative and passive-aggressive projections are non-verbal and include:

- ☐ Sulking
- ☐ Addictive behaviours such as overdrinking, overeating or starving oneself
- ☐ Physical withdrawal
- ☐ Emotional withdrawal
- ☐ Sexual withdrawal
- ☐ Hurting oneself (banging fist or head off solid object or, more seriously, cutting oneself or drug overdosing)
- ☐ Silence that may go on for weeks on end
- ☐ Damaging an item of value to the spouse

Examples of passive-manipulative or passive-aggressive verbal projections include:

- ☐ 'You don't love me anymore.'
- ☐ 'You wish I were dead.'
- ☐ 'I'll just pack up and go.'
- ☐ 'I'll kill myself.'
- ☐ 'I'll never open my mouth again.'
- ☐ 'I'll go home to mother.'
- ☐ 'I'll leave.'
- ☐ 'Isn't it better we part?'
- ☐ 'What's the use in talking?'

All of these messages – both non-verbal and verbal – indirectly blame the other person and the implied message is 'look at what you are driving me to do'. Such messages also have the subconscious purpose of making the other person feel bad and guilty in the hidden hope that he will change in behaviour towards the sender of the message. The messages involve no risk for the sender but they do involve risk for the receiver. If the receiver continues to pursue his right to have certain needs met – for example, to have some evenings free for self – he now risks coming home to a partner who is drunk or hostile, or who has taken a drug overdose. The strategy is extremely clever, but to give in to it means that both persons' individual development is blocked, huge resentment will develop in the receiver of the message, the relationship remains insecure and troubled, and the partner who is passive-aggressive remains stuck in her low self-esteem. What a price to pay!

It is important to see how projection actually protects the sender of the message. When a partner says, for example, 'you make me miserable', she loads all the responsibility for her feelings onto the other and takes no emotional risk in terms of failure, refusal or rejection. The message protects against any further threat to the self-worth of the sender. When the person sends a direct and clear

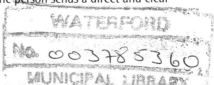

message such as, 'I feel lonely and miserable and I need us to talk about what is happening to our relationship', then the risk of rejection is greater. The vulnerable partner may respond with 'there's nothing to talk about', leaving the sender in an even more distressed state. The issue here is that the person who sends a blaming or manipulative message is not consciously trying to hurt or put down the other person but is attempting subconsciously to prevent any possibility of hurt or rejection.

It is a wonderful revelation to see that no matter what you say it is always something about yourself, even though it may appear to be about the other person. For example, if you say to your partner, 'you're always out', ask yourself, 'what is my hidden need in that criticism?' The answer you give yourself may be: 'he's never here when I want him' (still projecting). Ask yourself another question, 'what do I want of him?' Now the real issue is likely to emerge: 'well I would like help with the children at mealtimes and bedtimes.' This process has now led to a revelation of your own needs.

When a couple project onto each other they will see each other either as dominating, aggressive, controlling, blaming and critical or as passive, needy, manipulative, insecure and fretful. This type of communication inevitably leads to distancing within the couple relationship and further lowering of both persons' self-esteem levels and heightening of protectors.

Introjection is apparent where the person's identity is dependent on the feedback, opinions and reactions of others. Introjection occurs when the person receiving a message from another internalises the message as being about her rather than being about the sender. When the message is critical or abusive, the receiver will feel hurt, rejected and 'put down'. Likewise, the person who introjects a positive message sees the other as having greater knowledge about the receiver than does the receiver herself. The person who introjects and personalises what others say appears hypersensitive to criticism, easily hurt and vulnerable and as somebody in need of protection. The person's partner can respond to the need for protection by pussyfooting around or avoiding any confrontation with the person. Either of these protective reactions means that communication between the couple is vague or absent, with a consequent build-up of a whole range of unspoken and unmet needs.

Personalisation or introjection of a partner's behaviours arises from dependency on the other for acceptance, approval, affection and caring, with consequent fears of rejection, criticism, disapproval and failure. Dependency in turn is a product of poor acceptance and valuing of self (middle to low self-esteem), which itself originates in unresolved conflicts in childhood when either total neglect, emotionless parenting or conditional parenting left one feeling highly vulnerable. It is important to see this process clearly because reducing or overcoming introjection or projection is only possible when all the factors that have contributed to its development are perceived and worked upon. The figure below shows that the processes of projection and introjection are but the crest of a wave of an underlying sea of emotional experiences.

It is not difficult to see how projection protects the person from hurt and rejection but introjection too has a similar, if less easily observed, purpose. For example, if one partner says to another 'you're a fool' and the receiver personalises this by passively agreeing, the passive acceptance of the judgment protects from any further criticism, ridicule, hurt or rejection. Likewise, where the receiver personalises the message by attacking the partner, the aggressive retort protects by putting the spotlight back on to the

Introjection and projection

**Fears of rejection,
failure, criticism**

**Dependence on others
for acceptance and approval**

Middle to low self-esteem
(poor or no acceptance or love of self)

Unresolved childhood conflicts
(due to either parental neglect or conditional
or emotionless parenting/teaching)

partner who sent the message in the first place and off the receiver. Once the attention is off the receiver of the message, she has now managed to reduce the threat to self-worth. These ways of communicating are then best seen not as negative but as protective, and until self-worth begins to be realised, the partners in the couple will continue to employ such protective mechanisms.

In the German concentration camps during the Second World War some prisoners subconsciously began to walk like their German captors and even wore pieces of Nazi uniforms. This is an example of introjection where the person rationalises: 'if I become like the person who threatens me then he may not hurt me'. Individuals who continually try to please people take on the ideas, values, characteristics, opinions, dress and tastes of others in order to be accepted and valued. This attempt to please others reflects their own poor sense of self, their reliance on others for acceptance and love and their need to protect themselves from any hurt or rejection. Individuals who introject the other's message and then react aggressively, either by ridiculing or attempting to control the other person, are also showing a strongly guarded sense of self, dependence on others and a need to be accepted. The aggressive response may be an attempt to control the sender of the message so he cannot hurt the receiver of the message or it may be an effort to force the other person to accept the receiver of the message.

A surprising revelation for someone who introjects is that anything another person says is about that person and not about you. When you hear the other's message as being about you, you have totally misinterpreted the message: the focus now goes on yourself and, whether you passively withdraw or aggressively attack back, you have not heard the need of the sender and communication has broken down. If you had stayed separate from the sender's message and attempted to discover what it was saying about him, then communication would have stayed open and the chances of the sender having his need met would have been greater. To illustrate this process of overcoming introjection imagine someone says to you, 'you're so selfish'. Rather than hearing the message as being about you, you hear it as being about the sender, and you want to discover the hidden issue behind this blaming message. You return the message to the sender by saying: 'In what way do you feel I'm selfish?' The answer you get back will probably be another protective communication: 'You only think about yourself, never about me'. This statement, though still protective, is closer to the real issue and you now reply: 'In what way do I never think of you?' At this stage it is likely that the full hidden issue will begin to emerge: 'Well I feel you never notice when I'm tired or when I need help with cooking the meal, and you never ask me to go out with you'. Now you can respond: 'I wasn't aware you had those needs and I will do my best to notice in future. It does help though when you let me know what your needs are'.

In all cases where a person uses either projection or introjection she is revealing an absence of a valuing and accepting relationship with herself and, consequently, a deep dependence on the other. Until the former is resolved, the latter will persist.

Distance regulators

Distance regulators serve the function of avoiding emotional or sexual intimacy as these are felt to threaten the self-worth of the person. They may take the form of:

- □ Being busy
- □ Being absent
- □ Having 'no go' areas of conversation
- □ Involving a third party in the conflict
- □ Having frequent arguments over domestic affairs and responsibilities

The 'being busy' pattern, where one or both of the partners use work or some hobby or interest to fill all their time, is frequently seen. Being busy is a cleverly devised subconscious strategy to avoid emotional closeness because the risk of conflict is perceived as great when intimacy occurs.

'Being absent' can take the form of being thoroughly absorbed in some pursuit such as reading, watching television, house cleaning, gardening, car maintenance, child rearing and so on. The person is not 'tuned in' to her partner's life as this might further threaten self-worth and the relationship.

'No go' areas are common in situations where there is political conflict or social deprivation. 'No go' areas may also be present in a conflictual relationship. Examples are: 'don't talk about my family', 'don't mention closeness', 'don't bring up the topic of sex', 'keep my mother out of the conversation', 'never say anything about my job'. These 'no go' topics actually indicate the very areas in the relationship that need to be tackled but such openness and directness are not possible because of the vulnerability of each of the partners.

Triangulation is a very common development in problematic relationships. It refers to the situation where a third party is brought into the fray to serve the subconscious purpose of distracting the couple from their own conflict. A child can easily become the third party where one of the partners attempts to get some of his or her unmet emotional (and sometimes, sadly, sexual) needs met in the relationship with the child. This is illustrated in the triangle below where the father establishes a strong relationship with his daughter and excludes his wife, who then displaces her feelings of hurt, rejection and anger onto the daughter.

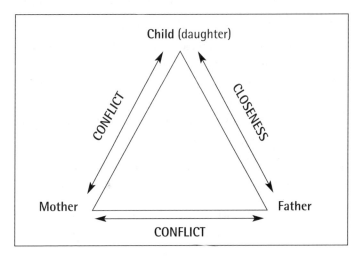

The following case is a typical example of triangulation. A neighbour had complained to a social worker of the likely victimisation of a five-year-old girl in a family of three other children. The mother frequently isolated this child from the rest of the family by sending her to a small backyard where she was forced to stand and look in on the rest of the family engaged in various activities. The father was upset by his wife's behaviour but he made no attempt to defend and protect his daughter even though he had a very close bond with her. It transpired that this close bond between father and daughter was the crux of the matter. The mother was very reluctant to seek help. She did not realise that her victimisation of her daughter was a displacement of her anger at feeling rejected and unwanted by her husband. She felt that the child was her husband's 'pet' and that she got far too much attention from him. The real issue was that she wanted that attention for herself but was afraid to ask for fear of rejection. What made her rejection of this child so strong was that when she was a child herself her father openly favoured a younger sister. It was as if she were experiencing the hurt and exclusion, felt back then, all over again.

It can be seen from this example that when triangulation occurs the third party can often become the target of attack and the real conflict issues between the parents are not faced. This is not deliberate behaviour on either partner's side but an unwitting attempt to protect against pain and rejection. Nonetheless, the tactic eventually results in other problems developing and in an escalation of the couple conflict.

Another frequent example of triangulation is where one of the partners has an extra-marital or extra-relationship affair.

For example, the wife takes a lover in order to have emotional and other needs met – needs which are not being recognised by an

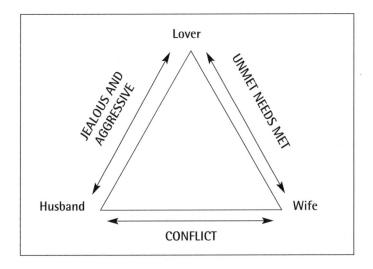

emotionless or a 'too busy' partner. She is too vulnerable to make emotional demands on her husband because of the risk of rejection. It seems easier not to confront and thus, unawares, she becomes open to an extramarital affair. All appears well until the affair becomes known. Now the husband will typically focus his attention on the lover but will not confront the real issue of the problematic relationship between him and his partner. Sometimes a passive partner may actually encourage the relationship as it means that the underlying conflict is totally avoided. In spite of the triangular situation neither partner may want to leave the other. Separation may occur if the lover pushes for a commitment and if it does, what results very often may be described as 'going from the frying pan into the fire'. A successful relationship depends on the high self-esteem of each of the partners. This will not have been established if one partner jumps from one relationship into another.

Another common distance regulator in problematic relationships is frequent petty disagreements over domestic issues such as who does the wash-up, who cooks, who gets the coal, who does the garden, who puts the child to bed. Petty disputes serve the purpose of screening the couple from deeper emotional issues which need to be tackled but which are too threatening to their individual sense of self to be voiced.

It is important to realise that partners in a relationship do not set out deliberately to hurt each other and their extreme behaviours are attempts to allay their worst fears about themselves as individuals. The more extreme the distance regulators, the greater the extent to which identity is tied to the relationship and the more protective the level of self-esteem. This does not mean that the behaviours of a problematic couple are justified. People are responsible for the consequences of their actions but they are not to blame – even when it comes to serious physical or sexual abuse. These are manifestations of extremely protective self-esteem and are examples of the third category of protective reactions, non-separation regulators.

Non-separation regulators

Non-separation regulators refer to attempts by one partner to tie the other to oneself by:

- Possessiveness
- Suicide threats
- Manipulation
- Aggression
- Suicide attempts
- Sickness
- Martyrdom
- Threats

The subconscious aim here is to make it virtually impossible for the other person to be either out of sight of or capable of doing without the partner.

The possessive partner constantly clings, needs reassurance, lives 'in the partner's pocket' and is easily upset when a need is not met. Very often, the possessive person's equally vulnerable partner will acquiesce to these high demands; he cannot do without a partner and even a suffocating relationship protects from having to face the lack of separate identity and high level of dependence. Thirteen per cent of widows and widowers die within six to twenty-four months of the death of the spouse. I have known couples who died within weeks, days and even hours of each other. It is as if when the spouse dies the remaining partner has no sense of self or of life without the couple relationship. As long as the protective behaviour of possessiveness works, neither partner will face the problematic nature of their relationship and their own individual vulnerability. The enmeshment of identity with intimacy is very obvious in such relationships. A person's identity can also be enmeshed with relationships other than with partners, or with an occupation or a favoured activity. For example, a bachelor can be overinvolved with an ageing mother, a career person can be overly dependent on occupation and an athlete can feel lost and at risk when no longer able to perform.

Aggression, like possessiveness, is also a means of binding one's partner to oneself. Any perceived slight or unmet need becomes magnified in the eyes of a partner with low self-esteem. Aggression is an attempt to make sure that needs are met and it protects against feelings of rejection when they are not. Again, a partner who is insecure and passive will go along with such extreme behaviours and even convince herself that the spouse cannot do without her. Attempts to persuade her by logic that she is allowing neglect by the other will be lost on her. There is a part of such people that believes that the violations are deserved and there is another part that is too terrified to separate out from even a violent partner. Only when her self-esteem has been elevated will she be able to confront the person who is protectively aggressive and decide to no longer accept the unhappy situation.

The 'martyr' spouse is the one who attempts to make herself indispensable to her partner. This person does everything for the partner and is very threatened when the partner attempts to do anything for himself. Again, the subtlety and cleverness of the strategy is commendable. By making yourself indispensable how could your partner ever leave you? Ingrid Bergman, the Swedish actress, once said of her first husband that he 'did everything for me and kept me totally helpless'. What she did not say is that at some preconscious level she allowed this dominance as it protected her from having to take responsibility for herself, a task she was not ready for at the time because of her own level of self-esteem.

Manipulation is yet another means of keeping a partner tied to oneself. Sexual manipulation is common in problematic relationships where sexual activity becomes a weapon to be wielded in the face of any threat to self-worth. Other means of manipulation include hostile silences, sulking, withdrawal, non-cooperation and suicide threats. All of these manipulative behaviours are directed at ensuring that the partner is always there for the other person so that that person is protected from any feelings of hurt or humiliation, or any possibility of the partner leaving.

Sickness can be an extreme form of manipulation. Here the person subconsciously becomes ill in order to tie the partner totally to oneself and to avoid the risk of rejection that comes from being active in the relationship. I recall one woman telling me how happy her husband was following a mild stroke that left him wheelchair-bound and totally in need of her care. Prior to this illness he was excessively threatened by any responsibility. Clearly, he could not live without her and his sickness made sure of her being life-bound to him.

THE EFFECTS OF COUPLE CONFLICT ON THE CHILDREN

Couple conflict blocks children's self-worth and their feelings of security but it does not always have to lead to family problems. Conflicting couples who stay together and whose children frequently witness 'scenes' between them have the most negative impact on children. The next most threatening situation is where the conflicting couple separate but the children continue to witness scenes between them. When parents choose to separate, the best situation for the children is where the parting is amicable and where the parents, though now separated, befriend each other and maintain close, loving relationships with their children. Of course, the ideal situation is where the couple resolve their conflicts, deepen their intimacy, establish their own separate identities and maintain loving relationships with each of the children.

Problems in children then are most likely to arise from intact conflictual couple relationships and broken but conflictual couple relationships. In younger children manifestations of problems are generally physical in nature:

- Bedwetting
- Hyperactivity
- Soiling
- Frequent infections
- Stammering
- Abdominal pains

- ☐ Thumb sucking
- ☐ Vomiting
- ☐ Physical withdrawal
- ☐ Psychogenic deafness
- ☐ Nail biting
- ☐ Asthma
- ☐ Clinging
- ☐ Other psychosomatic complaints

Abdominal pain in children is psychosomatic in 75 per cent of cases. When parents are in open conflict with each other, children become terrified that their needs for love and security will not be met and their bodies often mirror that hidden terror. Often children will develop physical ailments in order to distract the parents from the conflict between them. When the conflict is deep-seated the child can develop quite serious illnesses. The illness is really a symbol for the dis-ease between the parents. It also symbolises the child who is 'sick with fear' of not getting his needs met.

I recall being asked to see a child who had been complaining of severe abdominal pain since the age of three. She was now six and no organic reason for the pain could be found. Her appendix had been removed and was found to be perfect. The child's pain persisted after the operation and further exploratory surgery was suggested. I was told that the pain intensified at certain times of the year. Physical explanations had been suggested for this in terms of allergies or seasonal physical disorder. Nobody had checked what was happening psychologically and socially at these critical times. Severe pain began in mid-April and early September. Mid-April was the beginning of the tourist season and the time when her parents reopened their seasonal restaurant. Father felt he had to do everything and literally rushed, raced and shouted for the entire season. His wife worked equally hard but was nervous and anxious around her husband's irritability and bad temper. The child witnessed this scene day after day. Furthermore, she got little attention to her needs. She would not let her parents out of her sight during these months, her insecurity causing her to cling for fear of further loss. The pain also worsened in September when the child was due to go back to school. Separation from her parents, at the very time when the tourist season was ending and she might have had a chance to get her deepest needs met, was again a major threat and hence the increase in stomach pains. A child who is secure has little difficulty in separating out from parents and will willingly and joyfully return to school. A child, such as in this case, who is insecure in regard to herself and her parents' relationship and who feels threatened by parental neglect of her needs, finds any separation extremely difficult. The child's aunt told me that when she took her to school in the morning she could not even run into a shop to get a morning paper without the child bursting into tears; this reflected her very great fear of abandonment. In therapy the parents became aware of the effects of their own individual behaviour, as well as of their way of relating to each other, on the child's emotional and physical well-being. The removal of conflict between the parents and a greater focus on the needs of the child led to the gradual reduction and eventual disappearance of the pain symptoms.

Older children in distress tend to display behavioural or emotional rather than physical symptoms. Typical behavioural manifestations are:

☐ Stealing
☐ Boasting
☐ School phobia
☐ Absence from home
☐ Delinquency
☐ Attempting to please parents

- □ Temper tantrums all the time
- □ Bullying
- □ Learning difficulties

All these symptoms are subconscious attempts by the child to get conflicts, within self and between parents, seen and remedied. Unfortunately, such symptoms are often harshly dealt with, thereby plunging the child further into the shadows of low self-esteem. The problematic behaviours certainly need to be confronted but in a way that does not demean the child and the relationship between him and the parents. (Ways of responding constructively to problematic behaviour are discussed in Chapter 7.)

Children will do anything to keep parents together. Some children strive to be perfect in order to please parents and to make them happy and thus increase the likelihood of their staying together. These children often become the go-between when parents are in conflict, attempting to appease and comfort each parent following a row.

Children can also manifest emotional symptoms when parents are in conflict. Examples are:

- □ Timidity
- □ Frequent crying
- □ Shyness
- □ Apathy
- □ Emotional withdrawal
- □ Loss of motivation to do things
- □ Day-dreaming that were previously enjoyable
- □ Overabsorption with an activity
- □ Hopelessness

The greater the threat of the parental conflict to the child's emotional and physical well-being, the more frequent, intense and enduring these signs will be. It should come as no surprise that a child who witnesses frequent conflict between his parents will begin to fall behind in educational development. How can a child who is emotionally insecure and frightened attend to academic activities? Emotion is always stronger than cognition and such a child needs to have his emotional well-being tended to before he will begin to progress academically again. What is needed quickly is the absence of conflict.

RESOLVING COUPLE CONFLICT

When couples come to me one of my primary tasks is to help them see that they need to separate out from each other and realise that conflict will continue as long as the identity of each is tied to the relationship. The separation issue is connected with helping each of them to come to realise their own level of self-worth so that they can have greater independence of each other; can reduce the use of projection and introjection; and can develop open and relating ways of communication.

Separateness is an essential aspect of a successful couple relationship. The paradox is that the more separate and independent a person is, the greater and deeper can be the joining with another without loss of identity or individuality. An enmeshed relationship seriously blocks the unique identity of each person and the growth of individuality and independence. In an enmeshed relationship any attempt by one partner to become independent is viewed by the other as a threat to the relationship and to one's self-worth. Separateness is created through an intense, enduring, unconditional loving relationship with yourself. You cannot extricate yourself from enmeshment unless you first establish a safe and secure haven within yourself. Some people see separateness as not needing anyone but it is quite the contrary: many social, emotional, sexual, financial, intellectual, occupational and physical needs are met in relationships with partners, friends, families and colleagues. However, having a need is not a dependence. When a person is psychologically separate in a relationship, she will certainly express needs but will allow the other person the freedom to say 'yes' or 'no' to the expressed need. The person who is separate owns and takes responsibility for her needs. In a dependent relationship, a request becomes a command and a 'no' may be met with hostility, withdrawal, sulking, criticism and blaming.

Conflict can be a creative force within a relationship when it is seen as a signal for change both within the relationship and within the individual partners. No conflict would be present if no change were needed. Changing the protective and destructive aspects of a problematic relationship entails:

- realisation of self-worth by each partner (see Chapter 5)
- learning from projection and introjection (see pp. 117–20)
- establishment of open and relating patterns of communication (see pp. 45–6)
- development of an affirming relationship (see pp. 46–8).

COMMUNICATION AND THE COUPLE RELATIONSHIP

There are two main types of communication: open and protective. Unfortunately, the type of communication that is common in most couple relationships is protective communication, which creates relationship difficulties and increases the protective screen of each of the partners. As you read the descriptions below you may be surprised to discover how rarely you employ open or relating communication patterns and how frequently you use protective communication patterns.

Protective communication patterns

Protective patterns of communication block the fulfilment of needs and the expression of feelings and produce a circular reaction of further protectiveness. They lead to an unsupportive and threatening relationship. Protective communication takes many forms.

Judgmental messages

When a partner is being judgmental she accuses and criticises, which almost always results in a protective response in return from the other person such as withdrawal or criticism. Judging protects the partner from taking the risk of expressing her real needs and is an attempt to make the other person dependent on her. By making the other person dependent, the sender of the judgmental message protects against rejection or abandonment by the receiver of the judgmental message. When the person who receives the judgmental message either passively withdraws or criticises in turn, the sender of the message has achieved her purpose of attaining power over the other.

Examples of judgmental messages are:

- Criticising, name calling, characterising, blaming (for example, 'You're stupid', 'You never listen', 'You only think of yourself').
- Cross-examining, interrogating, fact-finding (for example, 'What exactly were you doing all day?', 'Who were you talking to on the phone?', 'I rang during the day and you were out, where were you?').
- Praising and approving (for example, 'That was a great meal', 'That suit looks A1 on you').

It may seem surprising that praising and approving can have blocking effects on relationships and on self-worth. When such messages are sent they are generally well intentioned (unless there is a hidden agenda, then they are manipulative) but, when they are phrased as in the examples above, they imply that the sender of the message can judge the other's performance. They also raise the possibility that the next performance may not reach the criteria for approval. The relationship created between the couple through this kind of communication is that of judge–supplicant. Does this mean that a person should never praise or approve of another's performance? Certainly not, but there are two issues which need to be taken into account here. First, it is always better to put the emphasis on effort rather than on performance, as every effort is an attainment. Second, praise or approval expressed in a judgmental way – for example, 'you're looking beautiful' – is best avoided because it expresses nothing about the sender and therefore is a protective message. Since all communications are about the sender, it is far more accurate when communicating that you are impressed, for example, by your partner's clothes, or a meal that she has cooked or a room that she has decorated to say: 'I particularly like that outfit on you', or 'I really enjoyed that meal' or 'I am impressed by the colour scheme you chose for the room'. The focus in these messages is on your perception and a particular aspect of the behaviour of the other and not on her person. To say 'you're looking beautiful' begs the question 'when don't I look beautiful?' When you communicate your message as being about you and your perception, you allow the other person to evaluate her own effort. It is often wise when you wish to communicate your perception of another's behaviour that you first check how that person sees it.

Controlling messages

When a person sends controlling messages she is being author-itarian, threatening and moralistic – all of which are likely to produce reactions of either flight or fight. Such messages will certainly lead to protectiveness on the part of the other, through either acquiescence or resistance, and there will always be resentment in the person who is vulnerable receiving the controlling message. The person who is controlling does not listen to the other's opinions or perceptions and discounts the other's feelings. Depending on the nature of the other person, these types of communication can produce either aggression or passivity, rebelliousness or acquiescence, fearfulness or authoritarianism. Controlling messages implicitly communicate that the other is unable to be responsible for himself and is in need of a controller. The controller, for her part, is attempting to protect against rejection but at the expense of the other. The person who controls others has middle to low self-esteem, believes subconsciously that nobody really wants her and attempts to gain some security by dominating her partner. Unfortunately, controlling communication undermines self-worth, creates distance in the couple relationship and does nothing for the self-development of the sender.

Examples of controlling messages are:

- Directing, commanding, ordering (for example, 'You'll do what I tell you', 'Just do it my way', 'You can't have your mother over', 'Your place is home here with the children').
- Warning, threatening, punishing (for example, 'I'm warning you not to bring up that issue again', 'Don't expect to see me here when you come home from visiting your friend', 'Don't touch me').
- Moralising, preaching (for example, 'A good mother wouldn't go back to work', 'What you need is some interest or hobby').

Strategic messages

In sending a strategic communication, the partner has hidden motivation – better known as a 'hidden agenda' – and is attempting to manipulate the other into meeting some hidden needs. Strategic communication is akin to emotional blackmail except that it happens at a hidden level. If the person receiving the message responds to the manipulation he will be strongly reinforced but, if he refuses to cooperate, outright rejection can speedily occur. The person who engages in strategic communication has middle to low self-esteem, otherwise she would be able to be open about needs and would willingly accept whatever reasonable response the other person may give. The strategy of the person who gives this kind of message is to reduce risk so that failure is minimised and no humiliation is experienced. However, this approach simply serves to maintain the self-esteem protectors of the sender of the message, it undermines the couple relationship – as no openness, trust or genuineness is shown – and it lowers the self-esteem of the other person.

Examples of strategic messages are:

- Non-verbal manipulation: sulking, physical or emotional withdrawal, hostile silences, sighing.
- Verbal manipulation (for example 'Darling, you'd do anything for me, wouldn't you?', 'Did you say you were going into town?' – where the hidden message is 'I need a message from the chemist').

Neutral messages

When a partner sends neutral messages she shows little concern for the other person. Somehow, the sender of the message is threatened by either emotional closeness or emotional conflict and neutrality protects against venturing into areas or ways of relating that threaten self-worth. Very often the other person manifests the 'being busy' syndrome to protect against hurt and rejection. Unfortunately, because the other does not read the sender's neurality as a protective strategy he can feel hurt, dismissed, unwanted and of little value. Once again, the self-esteem of both parties and the relationship between them is affected.

Examples of neutral messages are:

- ☐ Withdrawing, diverting (for example, 'I don't want to listen to that right now', 'Can we talk about something else?', 'I really have to go now').
- ☐ Ignoring, dismissing, responding 'on the run' (for example, 'I didn't hear what you said', 'Have you nothing better to talk about?', 'Can't stop to listen now, must run').
- ☐ Reassuring, excusing, consoling, sympathising (for example, 'You'll feel fine tomorrow', 'I'm sure you didn't realise what you were saying', 'There, there, stop the crying now', 'Don't I know how you feel').

Superior messages

In superior communication the message being sent is that 'I know best' or 'I am right' and 'if you follow what I say you won't go far wrong'. The partner who communicates in this way is, in reality, masking an inferiority complex. The compulsion to appear superior is an attempt to gain acceptance and approval from others and to protect against failure with its consequent humiliation and hurt. The problem with superior communication is that it deprives the other person of the worth-realising experience of solving his own problems. Superior communication also fosters dependence in the other person and it often leads to conflict (for example, the other person responds: 'don't tell me what to wear' to the superior message of 'you shouldn't wear blue, it doesn't look right on you'). A very wise rule of thumb is never to give advice to other people unless they first request it. When you give unsolicited advice it is likely to be heard as criticism and will produce a protective response of either criticism in return or silence.

Examples of superior messages are:

- ☐ Advising, recommending (for example, 'What you need to do is get up earlier each morning', 'Why don't you just leave him, he's no good anyway?').

▫ Diagnosing, psychoanalysing (for example, 'You're only saying that because you're tired', 'You're in bad form because your mother was here today, it happens every time', 'It's the job that's getting you down').

Certain messages

The pattern of certain communication is common in partners who hold very rigid attitudes and who tend to live their lives according to rules of 'should', 'should not', 'must', and 'ought to'. The need to be dogmatic and certain is again a subconscious means to gain acceptance and approval; to reveal any uncertainty or provisionalism in this person's eyes would be to show vulnerability and weakness and to risk disapproval and rejection. This type of communication does not value the other person's differences but emphasises instead his 'wrongness'. It invalidates his feelings and leads to a circular reaction of protectiveness and lack of openness.

Examples of certain messages are:

▫ Persuading (for example, 'Come on now, it has to be done').
▫ Lecturing (for example, 'The fact is men are stronger than women').
▫ Arguing (for example, 'I know I'm absolutely right about your father', 'Listen, there is no other way of looking at this issue', 'Don't contradict me').

All protective communication patterns reflect non-supportive couple (and other) relationships, where the self-worth of the partners is frequently threatened, leading to a lack of openness and trust. But the presence of protective communication patterns is a signal of the self-esteem protectors of the individual partners, and as such offers the opportunity for insight and change within and between the couple.

Open communication patterns

Open communication is exactly the opposite of protective communication.

PROTECTIVE COMMUNICATION	OPEN COMMUNICATION
☐ Judgmental	Non-judgmental
☐ Controlling	Permissive (allows the other person freedom to see and do things own way)
☐ Strategic	Spontaneous
☐ Neutral	Empathic (attempts to see and feel what the other person is experiencing)
☐ Superior	Equal (respects and listens to the other person's opinions and ways of doing things)
☐ Certain	Provisional (accepts that there may be an alternative answer or way)

Open or relating communication is essential for the fulfilment of individual and couple goals. It is a way of communicating where each partner experiences openness, intimacy and understanding with the other and where what is discussed is relevant and appropriate to each other's personal growth and the development of the relationship. For a couple to engage in this kind of communication each needs to have high self-esteem, to have a sense of adequacy and competency, and to trust in their ability to love, support and help each other. The partners also need to be aware of their own weaknesses and vulnerabilities, and to be able to be open about these when necessary. This kind of openness can only occur within a mutually supportive relationship.

It is vital for the individuals in a couple relationship (and in the family context) to practise communication patterns that create a positive, open, caring and trusting relationship. The key to a healthy couple relationship is that each partner works to establish a strong sense of personal worthiness, and creates a relationship between them that affirms, nurtures, and supports that process.

AFFIRMATION AND THE COUPLE RELATIONSHIP

Few people have reached the peaks of self-worth and the presence of affirmation in a couple relationship (or any relationship) aids the emergence of the self-worth of both individuals. Even when a partner has high self-esteem, affirmation is a bonus to be enjoyed. People have a need for recognition and approval. The difficulty arises when such needs become dependence since criticism or the absence of affirmation then becomes a severe blow to self-worth, which, in turn, badly affects the couple relationship. Recognition, respect, valuing, affirmation, praise and encouragement are not often regular features of interactions between couples. More common among couples are criticism, dismissal, avoidance, silence, non-listening and 'put-down' messages – all of which block self-worth and the couple relationship. It is the responsibility of both individuals in the couple relationship to develop the art of affirmation. Giving affirmation is a subtle, delicate matter but when it is done well it has many rewarding consequences. The following guidelines for giving affirmations may help you.

- *Only ever give honest and genuine affirmations.* If you are not genuine and sincere about the affirmation and you do not really feel that your partner deserves it, your non-verbal language (tone of voice, body posture, eye contact, facial expression) will give you away and your affirmation will be rejected as insincere.

- *Give the affirmation without expectation of a receptive response.* Generally, it is true to say that when a partner has difficulty in positively responding to an affirmation it means that he needs more affirmations. Do not give up; hold on to the fact that an affirmation is an expression of something you feel and perceive, and is not given to gain a particular response (otherwise it is manipulative). In the end the other person will see your genuineness and be affirmed by it.
- *The best affirmation is undivided attention to your partner.* Avoid effusive compliments which are rarely genuine. A look, a nod, a smile or a touch may be sufficient to affirm your partner. Always be sure to give your full attention.
- *Be sure the affirmation is unconditional and has no ulterior motive.* Do not give affirmation to get something back – such as an affirmation in return, praise or a favour – as this is manipulation and not affirmation.
- *Do not use clichés, jargon and popular superlatives* such as 'great', 'out of this world', 'A1', 'Fab', 'Super'. Be yourself and be genuine.
- *Spontaneous unconditional affirmations are the most powerful.*
- *Focus your affirmation and praise on an area that is important to your partner.* Look for signs from your partner of what is important to him. Possible areas are dress, work, house decor, garden, verbal language, interests, hobbies, reading, origin, education, music, literature, animals. Pay heed also to what you hear from his family, friends and colleagues.

Many people confuse affirmations with praise. An affirmation values some unique aspect of the person, such as his perception of things, or creative way of doing something, or dress sense, or good eye for colour, or unique way of looking, smiling and so on. Praise focuses on some action, such as clearing away after a meal, or cooking a meal, or decorating a room, or fixing a dysfunctional door, or mowing the lawn and so on. It is better to praise the effort in the action rather than the performance of the action.

KEY INSIGHTS

- Individuals bring their self-esteem protectors into the couple relationship and all the interactions between them are affected by their doubts, fears and insecurities.
- 'Problems marry problems'.
- A couple relationship can be a source of support, safety and encouragement for the development of each partner.
- No matter what people say or do they are revealing something about themselves.
- Individuals who continually try to please people take on the ideas, values, characteristics, opinions, dress and tastes of others in order to be accepted and valued.
- Couple conflict blocks children's self-worth and their feelings of security.
- Problems in children are most likely to arise from intact conflictual couple relationships and broken but conflictual couple relationships.
- Children will do anything to keep parents together.
- Children who come from homes where they witness frequent conflict between parents often make poor progress at school.
- Separateness is an essential aspect of a successful couple relationship.
- Conflict can be a creative force within a relationship when it is seen as a signal for change both within the relationship and within the individual partners.

- ☐ Protective communication patterns lead to unsupportive and threatening relationships between partners and between parents and children.

KEY ACTIONS

- ☐ Hear the other person's message as being about that person and not about you.
- ☐ Hear what you say as being about you and not about the other.
- ☐ Avoid persistent conflict with your partner and do not have scenes before your children.
- ☐ Practise communication patterns that create a positive, open, caring and trusting relationship.
- ☐ Develop the art of affirmation.

CHAPTER 3

LOVE AND YOUR CHILD'S SELF-WORTH

CONDITIONAL VERSUS UNCONDITIONAL LOVE

The major neurosis within Western society is dependence: dependence on performance – whether social, academic, work or sexual; on what others think or say about us; on physical appearance; on status; on having material things; on being valued, loved, accepted, praised and affirmed by others; and on success. The other side of the coin of dependence is fear: fear of failure; of making a fool of oneself; of new challenges and experiences; of not being liked, accepted, appreciated, affirmed and valued by others; of loss of status; of loss of material possessions; and of loss of face.

As mentioned earlier, the most common phobia is fear of public speaking. Ninety per cent of people avoid public speaking to protect themselves from any possibility of mistakes, failure, criticism or loss of face. People speak all the time but public speaking becomes fearful because of dependence on performance and approval. When people are forced into public speaking because of circumstances, such as a child's wedding, they can become highly anxious and may switch to perfectionism in order to reduce the risk of failure. Recall that perfectionism is a protective strategy whereby the individual overprepares for a task in order to ensure success and avoid the humiliation and embarrassment of failure. Likewise, when people are going for job interviews, or meeting new people, or going out on a date, or starting a new job, they may dread not being good enough to impress. How have all these doubts and dependencies come about? The answer lies primarily in the type of loving and caring received, initially within the family and later on within the classroom and school.

Love is either conditional or unconditional. Conditional love, the staple emotional diet of most family, school and other social systems, breeds multiple fears, dependencies and self-esteem protectors. People with moderate to high protectors will, unwittingly, be conditional within the systems in which they live and work.

Loving is conditional when it is used as a weapon within a social system. For example, where loving is conditional within families, love is given to or withdrawn from the family members depending on whether or not certain behaviours are present. You have seen that the children of teachers appear to be more at risk than children with parents in other professions. The reason for this is that teacher parents often put unreasonably high demands for academic perform-ance on their children. The reasoning seems to be: 'How could I as a teacher have a fool of a child?' Paradoxically, the parent is more likely to bring about that which is most feared by imposing such high demands for scholastic performance on the child.

The destructive power of conditional loving is illustrated in the life stories of many young people I have encountered. There was one young man who had got A grades all the way through college, up to his penultimate examination in his fourth year when he got a B. He was found drowned the morning following the announcement of the results. The condition operating for this young man was: 'If I don't get an A performance, I am worth nothing'. A fifteen-year-old boy told me that he had got 97 per cent in a mathematics test, and that, when he told his parents about his marvellous attainment, they both reacted crossly: 'What happened to the other 3 per cent?' I have worked with people of all ages who dread any prospect of failure and suffer a variety of psychosomatic illnesses such as ulcers, back pain, heart disease, migraine headaches and insomnia because of the conditions for love imposed on them during their childhoods.

There are many conditions for love other than academic performance which operate within families. Typical conditions for love, affection and affirmation include:

- Be good
- Behave
- Be perfect
- Be clever
- Be successful
- Be quiet
- Be like your brother (or sister)
- Be like me
- Be handsome
- Be beautiful
- Be sexy
- Be funny
- Be Catholic
- Be Irish
- Be conformist
- Be grateful
- Be the helper
- Be a good example

Person and behaviour are separate

Conditional love means that behaviour becomes more important than the person and the relationships between the members of the family. Every child, and also every adult, needs to loudly declare 'I am not my behaviour'. Most adults have difficulty in recognising and accepting that person and behaviour are separate. Typically, the value and worth of a person are judged through his behaviour. But being is there ever before behaviour. When you love a baby, it is the fact that your baby is unique, breathes, thinks and feels that leads you to love her. There are hardly enough behaviours being shown for you to say that you love the baby because she performs certain behaviours. It is vital to resolve the confusion between person and behaviour. Whether child or adult, people are always lovable and worthwhile in their person and nothing, not even the most despicable of behaviour, can take away from that unconditional positive regard.

At an earlier stage of my work, while I was involved in training counsellors in rape crisis centres, one of the counsellors expressed her hatred for the perpetrators. It was gently pointed out to her that if she hated the man or woman who engaged in sexual violations, how was she any different from the perpetrators? When you hate the person of anyone you are being emotionally neglectful of that person. I could well understand and accept the counsellor's hatred for the sexual violations but not for the person. I am very clear with individuals who have physically, sexually or emotionally neglected children, adolescents or adults that I totally abhor what they have done and that responsibility has to be taken for the neglect that has been perpetrated. But, I also let them know that I love and respect their person and that I know what they have done is due to the fact that their person as a child was violated by other adults who, unfortunately, knew no better. The only possibility for healing people who have hurt others or themselves is to love them deeply and unconditionally.

No piece of behaviour is ever worthy of breaking a relationship. People often break relationships with others, whether with children, partners, lovers, work colleagues or neighbours, at the drop of a hat. For example, someone says 'you promised to call and you never did, well that's the last I want to see of you' – all because someone did not phone. What a heavy price to pay for a little misdemeanour! Such dismissal of relationships because of difficult behaviour is all too common within families, classrooms, workplaces, churches – in fact, within all social systems. Problematic behaviours, whether they be of a minor or serious nature, need to be confronted and responsibility has to be demanded but without threatening the relationship with the perpetrators of the problematic behaviour.

The potentially blocking effects of conditional love even with very young children is illustrated in the following case of a young mother and her two-year-old daughter. This mother reacted to any misdemeanour of the child by withdrawing all attention from her and not talking to her, sometimes for days or weeks or even months. The child came to my attention through a caring teacher who spotted that she was terrified of making the least mistake. The child's fear of mistakes was not surprising as when she did make one her whole world fell apart. The withdrawal of parental love is the most devastating experience for a child. This child had learnt to go to the extremes of perfectionism in order to hold her mother's attention. The cost was great in terms of chronic fear, timidity, and endless attempts to please mother and other people. The child's mother had not realised the neglect she was causing and was very willing to work on her own problems in order to change her relationship with her child and to reduce the emotional pressures within herself.

Behaviour is the means by which you explore, experience and learn about the world; it does not add one jot to your worth as a person. If you think your behaviour reflects your worth then you are dependent, trapped and conditional with yourself and you will also unwittingly project that onto others. For example, if I believe that being a clinical psychologist makes me important and valued, in my own eyes and in the eyes of others, then I am highly vulnerable to criticism, loss of status, retirement or loss of work. Research has shown that a high percentage of people die within a couple of years of retiring from their occupations. If people find their value through their work they are vulnerable. When that source is gone they may lapse into hopelessness, which is now known to have a highly debilitating effect on the immune system.

Enjoy your behaviour, be challenged by it, learn and grow in knowledge and wisdom through it, but do not be ruled by it. Constantly keep in mind that your worth and value as a person are always separate from anything you do, say, think, dream or feel. You can always improve your behaviour but never your person, which is perfect and unique.

Comparisons are acts of rejection

Another way in which conditional love operates within a family system is where comparisons are made between one member and another or between family members and outsiders. An act of comparison is an act of rejection, because it is saying that the person as he is now is not acceptable, but (here comes the condition) if he were like the other person, then he would be acceptable. Comparisons within the family and with others are common. Comparisons are sadly even more prevalent within classrooms and workplaces. A distinction needs to be made between skills and attributes: it is okay to admire and want to emulate certain skills or behaviours other people display – but not their attributes. Examples of skills or behaviours that you may see in another and perhaps would like to develop for yourself are: driving, gardening, woodwork, decorating, dress sense and so on. Acquiring these skills does not in any way add to your worth as a person and, once you realise that, you can learn

a lot from another person's way of doing things. Examples of attributes, which are characteristics unique to each person, are: height, hair
colour, eye colour, body shape, skin texture and so on. In the case of
an attribute, when a man, for example, desires to be as handsome or
as tall or as slim as another, he is comparing himself to another and
by that very action rejecting himself. Often people will go to the
extreme of surgery to 'fix' the unacceptable part but all the time they
are in a vicious circle of rejecting themselves. It is also a bottomless
pit because when you 'fix' one part you want to then 'correct' other
parts. You may also dread any deterioration in the 'fixed' part.

Unconditional love and responsibility

Unconditional loving not only means acceptance, care, affirmation
and the absence of comparisons but also encouragement of
behaviours that build competence while keeping behaviour and
person separate. For example, your son does his home exercises
and presents them to you for inspection but he has rushed doing
them and the results are fairly illegible and mostly inaccurate. You
want to correct the child's irresponsible behaviour of rushing and
carelessness without in any way threatening his self-worth or your
relationship with him. An altogether too typical reaction would be
'that's a mess, do it again', or 'you're just a lazy messer and you are
not going out to play until that exercise is done properly'. Both of
these messages lessen the child's sense of self. The first message is
judgmental and does not teach the child anything while the
second message labels and puts down the child and again does not
help the child grow from the experience of a poor level of effort.
If you want to improve your child's level of responsible effort and
maintain his self-worth, ask him firstly how he himself sees his
completed exercise and whether he believes you or the teacher
would be happy with his effort. Let him know that you believe he

can make a greater effort than he has done. Parents tend not to talk to children, but instead to direct, command, advise, scold, correct, judge and label them. Parents do not often engage children in giving their point of view but, if you do, you will find that your child knows when he has been attempting to slide out of responsibility in order to engage in more pleasurable behaviours like playing with friends and so on. Let him know you understand his need to play but you would not be loving him if you allowed him to get away with being irresponsible. When, with your help, he has completed his school task with genuine care and effort, he can go out to play but not until then. This may seem to be an elaborate way to correct a child's behaviour but the benefits are great: the child's self-worth remains intact, your relationship with him is enhanced and you have helped him to see where his responsibility lies.

Generally, when you want to encourage responsible 'good' behaviours it is important to avoid messages such as 'you're a good person' or 'you're a good boy'. The implication of these is that the goodness of the person is tied up with a particular responsible action and is dependent upon its presence. It is better to praise the particular action that has impressed you. For example, instead of saying 'you're a good boy' it is more valuable for the child's self-worth to say 'I was pleased when you noticed I was tired and you helped me clear the kitchen table after dinner'. Of course, you want to let your child know that he is always good, worthy and valuable in your eyes and the medium for this enduring, unconditional message is the relationship that exists between you and the child. Regrettably, the ways of relating in families and other social systems are often either grossly neglectful or conditional: they are rarely unconditional.

FAMILY COMMUNICATION AND SELF-ESTEEM

Communication is about needs

Communication is the means through which family members let each other know about their physical, psychological and social needs. It can be both verbal and non-verbal. Babies usually communicate their needs by crying, banging their heads, making noise, wriggling their bodies and so on. Of course many adults may also use such means to express needs!

It is interesting that babies in Java rarely cry whereas crying is very common among babies in Western culture. Research has shown that in Western society babies, on average, cry for thirty minutes before they get a response. There is a misguided notion that picking up children when they cry serves to reinforce and increase the crying but nothing is further from the truth. Most parents know that babies give a different type of cry for different types of needs: they have a particular cry when they are in pain, a different cry when they are hungry and a different cry when they need affection. The crying is only a symptom of a need; when the need is met the crying reduces not increases. Parents are also aware of the 'pseudo' cry when the child wants attention all the time and this kind of 'crying' does not need an immediate response. It appears that in Java the parents pick up earlier and different signals of need from their babies before they have to resort to crying. A Javanese baby is never allowed to touch the ground for the first six months of life and the close contact between the child's and the parent's body enables earlier detection of needs. In this situation, needs, particularly love needs, are being regularly met whereas Western babies have to shout and scream to get such attention. It is important within families to try to pick up the non-verbal signals of need. This is essential up to the time of language development but even afterwards such sensitivity is wise and caring.

The primary function of the family is to facilitate the optimum devel-opment of each family member, and this means being responsive to the whole host of needs which each person experiences. It may not always be possible to meet certain needs but the expression of all needs can be both actively encouraged and modelled by parents. When parents themselves do not communicate clearly with each other about their needs or when one or both do not feel worthy to even express their needs, never mind having them met, then it is unlikely that the children of these parents will learn to talk about their needs.

There are many needs which each person within a family may experience:

□ Emotional
□ Occupational
□ Social
□ Financial
□ Intellectual
□ Recreational
□ Sexual
□ Spiritual
□ Sensual
□ Physical
□ Behavioural
□ Material
□ Creative

Asking for what you want

There are four ways in which family members can verbally express their needs:

- directly and clearly
- indirectly but clearly
- directly but unclearly
- indirectly and unclearly.

In effectively functioning families direct and clear communication is common whereas in ineffective or dysfunctional families one of the other three types of communication or some combination of them is the more frequent mode of expression of needs.

Direct and clear communication

If, for example, you want to communicate directly and clearly an emotional need to be embraced by your partner then you might say: 'Helen, I am feeling vulnerable and need to be held', or 'Helen, I'm feeling loving and would like to embrace you'. The message is direct because it is addressed to Helen and it is clear because it spells out how you are feeling and what your need is. The expression of sexual needs in particular is difficult for many couples because a refusal by the partner is seen as rejection and becomes a threat to self-worth. A partner or lover beats about the bush saying, for example 'are you staying up late tonight?', or 'are you feeling tired?', or 'will we have an early night?' It may feel too risky to say directly and clearly, 'John, I feel like making love with you now', or 'Margaret, I'm feeling incredibly sexy and would love to make love with you'.

Even more difficulties may arise when someone is feeling angry or upset about some unmet need and wants to communicate this dissatisfaction to a partner, friend or child. For example, if your partner continually turns up late for meal times and you greet him with a burnt dinner, a hostile silence, a sulking face, a blaming statement ('you're always late'), or a cynical or sarcastic remark ('I suppose you've had another busy day'), it is unlikely that your need for your partner to be on time for meals will be met. Each of these responses will lead to some defensive reaction on the part of the person addressed. He may just say nothing and emotionally withdraw, or may retort with some remark such as 'you're always complaining', or 'why would I want to come home to such abuse?' Both partners now end up hurt and humiliated, communication has broken down, self-worth has been threatened and the relationship is strained. Your communication will be clear and direct if you can own your need and say: 'John, when you are late for meals I feel frustrated and unappreciated and I need you to be on time or at least let me know when you are going to be late.'

The more children observe their parents expressing their needs directly and openly the more they will learn to do so as well. It is important that adults and children alike realise that a request to have a need met is not a command. However, if needs are regularly not being responded to, then some definite action is needed on the part of the person experiencing the unmet needs. Adults can and are required to take responsibility for getting their needs met. But children have many needs that they cannot meet by themselves and they are therefore highly dependent on the adults who take care of them. This makes young children much more vulnerable than adults and, to a lesser degree, than adolescents. Where children's needs are continually disregarded, the action needed to redress the situation may have to be initiated by someone outside the family as the children cannot do this for themselves.

Indirect but clear communication

Where communication is indirect but clear there is still the likelihood that needs will go unmet but the danger is less than with direct but unclear or indirect and unclear patterns of communication. In indirect but clear communication the person for whom the request or statement is intended is not directly addressed. Some examples of indirect but clear messages are:

- ☐ 'Nobody ever notices when I feel vulnerable and need some attention.'
- ☐ 'I'm really feeling very sexy.'
- ☐ 'Nobody does anything around here but me.'
- ☐ 'People who make decisions about other people's work make me angry.'
- ☐ 'The children are getting me down.'

The messages are quite clear but the problem is that they are not directed to any one person, and certainly not to the person for whom they are directly intended. Very often, the sender of these messages does not feel listened to but there is no indication in the message of who is to listen.

There is a protective purpose in sending an indirect but clear message: by not directing your request to any one person you avoid the possibility of refusal or rejection. This strategy is subconscious but it is a clever way to protect yourself from hurt or humiliation. Unless you learn not to personalise the other person's behaviour and to increase your own sense of self-worth it is unlikely that you will be able to take the risk of direct and clear communication.

Because the message is clear the sender may get some of his needs met by a discerning and sensitive listener. However, there will be many unmet needs as well. The person who engages in this type of communication is likely to have middle to high self-esteem and, generally, some gentle confrontation will lead to more direct messages.

If you notice your child using this type of communication, see it as one indication of a developing self-esteem problem. It is important to help the child to communicate directly and clearly but it is even more important to pay attention to the emergence of her self-worth.

Direct but unclear communication

Direct but unclear communication is the most common means of expressing needs. This kind of communication is typified in the 'you' messages given in the following examples:

- □ 'You're always late.'
- □ 'You only think of yourself.'
- □ 'You're so aggressive.'
- □ 'You think you know it all.'
- □ 'You're a fool.'
- □ 'You think you're perfect.'
- □ 'You look beautiful.'
- □ 'You did well.'
- □ 'You're a hopeless case.'
- □ 'You're lazy.'
- □ 'You're always out.'

The problem with 'you' messages is that they say absolutely nothing about the sender or the sender's needs. They also judge, 'put down' or blame the other person, which generally leads him to withdraw or attack back. Typical responses to the above examples are:

- □ 'So what?'
- □ 'Who else is going to think of me?'
- □ 'I'd need to be to get anything done around here.'
- □ 'Well I certainly know more than you do.'
- □ 'You're right I'm a fool to listen to you.'
- □ 'Well you're certainly not.'
- □ 'Do I really?'
- □ 'Do you think so?'

- ☐ 'You're so negative, how could I learn anything from you?'
- ☐ 'Always the bad word.'
- ☐ 'Well why would I want to be in?'

Because the messages are unclear and because they blame the other person, there is little likelihood of getting your hidden, unrevealed needs met. It is easy to see how the blaming 'you' message, even though it protects the sender, leads to a quick breakdown of communication between sender and receiver, whether between parent and parent, parent and child or child and child. It is less apparent how the praising/affirming 'you' message can lead to self-esteem protectors but it does so nevertheless. When you say to your child 'you're a good girl', once again you reveal nothing of yourself and you set yourself up as judge of another person's actions. The danger here is that the child will learn that the way to please you is through her actions. A more accurate message to send is: 'I am impressed by that piece of work and I'd like to know how you feel about it?'

Direct but unclear communication may be regarded as negative but it serves a very useful purpose, which is to protect the sender from criticism and rejection. By putting all the responsibility for the situation onto the other person (for example, 'you're so insensitive') the sender of the message takes no risk; he is not revealing any need and is not making any request. This type of protective communication is used by people with low to middle self-esteem. The influence of self-esteem is pervasive and affects all your actions whether these be towards yourself, towards other adults or towards your children. When you have a poor sense of your own value as a person, unwittingly you will use unclear means of communicating your needs, even to your own children, and they, in turn, will develop the same apparently low-risk communication strategies.

Indirect and unclear communication

Indirect and unclear communication is the most protective kind; it seriously blocks the self-worth of the person receiving the message and leads to an immediate breakdown in communication. Cynicism and sarcasm typify indirect and unclear communication and their use reveals the low self-esteem of the sender of the message.

Cynicism and sarcasm focus all the attention on the person to whom the message is addressed and, cleverly, take all the attention off the sender. There is no risk of rejection for you when you send such messages but your needs will not be met as nobody will have a notion of what your needs are. For example, feeling lonely and in need of company and closeness, you say, 'you might as well be in a graveyard as living in this house'. This message is upsetting for anyone listening as it is highly critical and it is indirect because no one person has been addressed. Most of all, nobody has a notion of what you are really talking about and, in addition, they are probably busy protecting themselves or backing off from such a 'put-down' message.

Many children are victims of sarcasm and cynicism within homes and classrooms. This form of communication closes the door on a child's self-worth and may also lead to the child using this type of communication. The child has no idea what the parents or teachers need from her when they use indirect and unclear communication. Examples of this kind of communication are:

- □ 'Here comes Mammy's little boy.'
- □ 'Is there a mouse in this house?'
- □ 'Look at the face of it!'
- □ 'I might as well be talking to the wall.'
- □ 'Is everybody blind in this house?'
- □ 'What kind of donkeys have we got in this class?'

Children need to be helped and encouraged to express all their needs directly and clearly. When a child uses any of the other three types of communication patterns it means that she feels threatened by the response of the parent or teacher and so to avoid possible criticism, humiliation and rejection, she uses a protective means of expressing needs. It is vital that a parent notices when this symptom of the child's self-esteem protectors occurs, so that immediate and continuous corrective action can be taken. It is also important that children are aided to observe and respond positively to the reasonable requests of parents and other adults. Children tend to believe the world revolves around them and, even when it clearly does not, they still think it ought to. They need to be helped to see they are not the only ones with needs within the family and that each person's reasonable needs are accepted and responded to when possible.

Confrontation on unmet needs

Many of us turn a blind eye when we witness children or adults being neglected and violated. We rationalise that it is not our place to interfere. There may be some grounds for such a rationalisation in the case of adults but where children are concerned no excuse is strong enough for failure to act. There are many families where an adult – parent, relative or outsider – witnesses children being hurt, humiliated, physically and even sexually violated but nothing is done. So many unmet needs of children have gone unconfronted under the banner, 'for peace sake, don't upset your father (or mother)'. I am also aware of teachers who see children being unjustly criticised, scolded, ridiculed and even physically hit by a colleague in school but they do nothing. The reason for inaction lies in the witness's own protective self-esteem and his fear of the response to the confrontation from the offending person. The problem is that everybody loses out when neglected needs are not confronted. Clearly, the parent or teacher or other significant adult who mistreats a child or partner or colleague is in need of professional help, and failure to confront the neglect or mistreatment leads to perpetuation or even worsening of his problems. On the other hand, the persons who are neglected develop a screen self due to feeling unwanted, unloved and not good enough. When there are children involved, they learn to imitate the blocking behaviours of the person who is neglectful and so the whole cycle repeats itself in their lives. Everybody loses out when confrontation of unmet needs does not occur within families. No change is now possible, and the sad process of gross emotional neglect, conditional loving, or physical or sexual violation continues, blocking the mature development of each member of the family.

Confrontation is not blaming; if it takes the form of blaming it leads to an exacerbation of the problems being addressed. Confrontation involves the direct and clear expression by a member of the family of his unmet needs. It cannot be an attack on the other person as this attack assumes that the other person is deliberately neglecting her partner, child, friend, relative or colleague. This is not only a gross assumption but also a judgment and a criticism, and will lead to a strong defensive action on the part of the person attacked. People do not intentionally violate each other; but to protect themselves from hurt and rejection they subconsciously resort to a range of behaviours that lead, unfortunately, to the other person being ignored, dismissed, neglected, judged, criticised, ridiculed and so on. The following examples clarify the process.

Take a husband who is possessive, controlling and dominating. This man's wife is blocked from meeting her needs to be free, to be different, to make her own friends, to develop her career and so on. His 'blocking' behaviours are not there to prevent his wife from developing her own identity and life-path but serve as an insurance against her leaving him. Subconsciously this man believes that he is not worthy enough in his own right to hold his wife.

I recall one married woman who came for help. She had been married for fifteen years and during all those years she had allowed her husband to dominate virtually every aspect of her life. He would not allow her to bring friends into the house; she could not wear clothes or make-up that emphasised her figure and features; he prevented her from taking up a part-time job; and he insisted that he always go shopping with her. When they went out socially he would cling to her side all evening, and if she were gone to the ladies' room for longer than five minutes there would be an interrogation on her return. She was highly critical and blaming of him and claimed that he was ruining her life. When it was gently pointed out to her that she was an adult and it was she who was ruining her own life by giving her husband so much power, she was dismayed and said she had never looked at it in this way before. This was wisely protective of herself because, like her husband, she had very low self-esteem and deep down did not believe she could cope on her own. Through guidance she was helped to elevate her self-esteem and resolve her childhood conflicts, and she was then taught to confront her husband on his possessiveness.

The first step in confrontation is verbal and involves:

- direct communication (using the person's name)
- an 'I' message
- declaration of how you feel
- expression of your needs.

Using these guidelines, the woman's message to her husband was: 'Michael, when you criticise my friends and my clothes and insist on going everywhere with me, I feel suffocated; I need to be able to choose my own friends, clothes and go out on my own at times'. As might be predicted, this message terrified her husband leading to an increase in his attempts to control her. She had been warned of this outcome; confrontation was likely to weaken the protective weapon of her husband and, initially, he was likely to wield it all the more in the hope of regaining power. She then had to go beyond verbal confrontation to the level of active confrontation. All the words in the world are not strong enough to combat another person's deep insecurity but actions always speak louder than words. The actions advised were to wear make-up as she chose, to wear clothes that she liked, to invite friends in, and at times to go shopping on her own. She also got a part-time job. She was further counselled not to get into verbal conflict with her husband as this could become a means of control in one or the other's hands. She was entitled to do the things she was doing and did not need the 'permission' of her husband. He continued to rant and rave for some time but gradually those reactions died down when he saw they were not gaining him any ground. Eventually he came for help and it quickly became evident why his behaviours had been so extreme. He had no sense of himself at all, he saw himself as 'nothing' and he truly believed that if any man even winked in his wife's direction she would be gone, as he could not really understand what she saw in himself. Both of them are now stronger in themselves, more independent in their relationship with each other and closer emotionally and sexually with each other. Clearly confrontation can be a creative force for all members of a family. However its absence leads to a spiralling of problems.

Children are in a much weaker position when it comes to confrontation and they have to depend on adults to take up their cause for them. However, they are frequently let down in this regard. Children are always victims but they do not see this; more often than not children blame themselves for their parents' coping problems and will label themselves as 'bad', 'dirty', 'stupid', 'unlovable', 'ugly' and so on. It has already been pointed out that parents or other adults are not to blame for the neglect they perpetuate on children. But, though not to blame, they are responsible for the consequences of their behaviours and need to be firmly encouraged to undo what harm they have done. If they refuse to take responsibility, then strong action is needed on the part of other adults to ensure that the children involved are no longer neglected. My own experience is that people who have been neglecting or violating children respond positively to sensitive and caring but firm confrontation. Those who resist have been badly neglected themselves, and strong action is needed to protect children from these adults, who are in great need of help themselves. But coercion of adults to take psychological and social counselling rarely works. In any case, coercion is an aggressive action and is not an appropriate means of confrontation.

Sometimes a partner or parent or teacher will come to my office and blame me for the consequences of active confrontation by somebody in their lives. The following are some examples:

- 'You've changed my life.'
- 'You've put me out of my own home' (barring order).
- 'You've taken my child from me' (child in care).
- 'How dare you remove a child from my class?'

I point out to those who blame me that the actions taken are not at all designed to get at them but to protect the children or adults who have been neglected or abused. I also point out that when they are ready to accept responsibility for their negligence and when they are able to change to being caring of those who have been hurt, humiliated and blocked then the whole situation can be reviewed.

KEY INSIGHTS

- ☐ The major neurosis within Western society is dependence.
- ☐ Conditional loving breeds multiple fears, dependencies and self-esteem protectors within children.
- ☐ Conditional love means that behaviour becomes more important than the person and the relationship between the members of the family.
- ☐ Person and behaviour are separate.
- ☐ No piece of behaviour is ever worthy of breaking a relationship.
- ☐ An act of comparison is an act of rejection.
- ☐ Unconditionally loving children and teaching children to be responsible go hand in hand.
- ☐ Many unmet needs of children have gone unconfronted under the banner, 'for peace sake don't upset your father (or mother)'.
- ☐ Actions always speak louder than words in situations of confrontation.
- ☐ Children frequently blame themselves for their parents' problems.

KEY ACTIONS

- ☐ Do not confuse the person of a child with her behaviour, no matter how difficult the latter may sometimes be.
- ☐ Love your children for themselves and not for what they do.
- ☐ Practise direct and clear ways of communicating with your partner and children.
- ☐ Ensure that constructive confrontation on unmet needs is a regular feature of family life.

CHAPTER 4

BEHAVIOURAL CONTROL AND YOUR CHILD'S SELF-WORTH

BEHAVIOURAL CONTROL IS NOT JUST FOR CHILDREN

The term behavioural control refers to the pattern of responses a family adopts for dealing with behaviour in the following three specific situations:

- physically dangerous situations
- situations which involve expressing and addressing psychobiological needs and drives (for example, eating, sleeping, drinking, eliminating, sexual activity)
- situations involving personal and social interactions both inside and outside the family.

It has to be emphasised that the topic of behavioural control does not refer just to the management of children but also includes consideration of how parents take control of their own behaviours in these three areas. Examples of physically dangerous situations for children include stairways, busy roadways, dangerous play areas, fireplaces. On the part of parents, examples of out-of-control behaviours which need to be managed include dangerous driving, violence and suicide attempts. Likewise, with regard to psychobiological drives, adults need to model management of behaviour before they can expect children to do so. For example, wolfing down food, overeating, excessive drinking, sexual promiscuity, 'taking to the bed', are all areas where adults need to take control of their behaviour. Children imitate their parents, particularly their actions, and adult words often fall on deaf ears of children when the words do not match the parents' actions. Similarly, responsible social behaviour both within and outside the family needs to start with the parents. The distinction between behaviour inside and outside the family is an important one; what is acceptable within the home may not be tolerated outside the home. In addition, sometimes a child can be a 'street angel' but a 'house devil' and vice versa.

Behavioural control starts with the parents. The parent who frequently loses control in relation to a partner, other adult or child is hardly in a position to demand that others control themselves. The parent has the responsibility to be in control of herself and any loss of control with children is an abrogation of that responsibility.

The parent who is out of control and responds critically and aggressively to the children is, in fact, giving the children control over her. In such a family, the children know that they can 'get at' the parent and, since children are not given a lot of power in the home, this bit of power becomes a weapon to be employed, particularly when their self-worth is under threat. Sometimes, children's behaviour can be extremely exasperating and the parents' responsibility to stay in control of their behaviour may be severely tested. When such a situation occurs for you it is always best to remove yourself from the child. The last thing you want is to add fuel to the fire of the situation. An aggressive response will breed either more unacceptable behaviour or withdrawal on the part of the child, and it will certainly affect the relationship between you. Parents who find it difficult to control their appetite behaviours (eating, drinking) or critical and aggressive responses to their children or irresponsible actions of neglect clearly have

EXAMPLES OF 'OUT-OF-CONTROL' BEHAVIOURS OF PARENTS WITHIN THE HOME

- ☐ Shouting at children
- ☐ Ordering, dominating and controlling children
- ☐ Using sarcasm and cynicism as means of control
- ☐ Ridiculing, scolding, criticising
- ☐ Labelling children as 'bold', 'stubborn', 'stupid', 'lazy', 'no good'
- ☐ Threatening children that the parent will leave them
- ☐ Threatening to send children away
- ☐ Physically threatening children
- ☐ Being physically violent
- ☐ Assigning punishments out of proportion to misdemeanours
- ☐ Pushing, pulling and shoving children
- ☐ Comparing one child with another
- ☐ Having an obvious favourite in the family
- ☐ Not calling children by their first names
- ☐ Being too strict
- ☐ Expecting too much of children
- ☐ Showing no interest in children's welfare
- ☐ Letting children slide out of responsibility
- ☐ Not showing affection to children
- ☐ Punishing mistakes and failures
- ☐ Never apologising for mistakes
- ☐ Not saying 'please' and 'thank you' to children
- ☐ Being inconsistent and unpredictable in response to children's irresponsible behaviours
- ☐ Allowing the children to control the parent
- ☐ Spoiling and overindulging children
- ☐ Withdrawing love from children
- ☐ Using hostile silences to attempt to control children

self-esteem problems and are in need of professional help. It is the responsibility of these troubled parents to seek help to resolve their difficulties so that they do not pass on their emotional and behavioural baggage to their children. Parenting classes are now readily available, as are individual and parent counselling services. There are also many books, audio and video tapes available to aid parents with their own personal, interpersonal and child-rearing responsibilities.

CONTROL OF CHILDREN IS NOT THE PARENTS' RESPONSIBILITY

It is not the parents' job to control their children whether inside or outside the home! This view is likely to be contrary to your own experience as a child and to what most parents believe. However, a closer look at traditional discipline practices reveals that to get one person to control another is a recipe for conflict. As an adult you know that you react defensively when another person attempts to dominate you or tells you what to do, where to go, what to wear, what to say, what not to say, how to stand, how to sit and so on. In such situations, either you feel hurt or helpless and stay silent, or you feel angry and you 'lash' back at the person. The same holds for children and adolescents. Effective behavioural control within a family is based on the principle that members of the family are responsible for their own self-control. It is not then the job of parents to control children since it is the responsibility of children to control themselves. However, it is the responsibility of parents to educate children to take responsibility for themselves.

In the family, each member has certain responsibilities to ensure that order, safety, fairness, caring, justice and harmony are developed. Abrogation of these responsibilities by children is best not met by a domineering critical response from the parents but by sanctions.

Drunken driving has been considerably reduced in this country due to an increase in sanctions against it. The sanctions are there to ensure responsible social behaviour. When an individual chooses to be irresponsible she also chooses the sanction. Many adults and children try to blame others (policemen, traffic wardens, parents, teachers) for the sanction but it needs to be firmly pointed out that no sanction would have occurred if a responsible choice had been taken. Children learn quickly that responsible behaviour gains them privileges and irresponsible actions lose them privileges. Children also begin to realise that it is they who choose the risk of sanction when they act in difficult ways. A sanction need never involve the withdrawal of love and respect; the relationship needs always to remain paramount.

Within the family the responsibilities of children need to be clearly spelt out. Once a child has attained a good level of language development many issues related to the management of certain behaviours can be verbally explained. Before that stage of language development, non-verbal responses to children's out-of-control behaviours are equally effective. For example, if your two-year-old child attempts to get her own way by throwing a temper tantrum then she can be given the sanction of lack of attention to her behaviour and failure to gain whatever the desired response was from you (such as sweets before dinner). Because you remain calm and do not lose control, you maintain your unconditional loving relationship with the child, while letting her know (through inaction on your part) that that type of behaviour will gain her nothing.

With children who can read it is a good idea to have a typed list of their responsibilities within the home. It is desirable to include older children in drawing up and reviewing such a list. The list of responsibilities needs to clearly specify what the sanctions are when a child fails to meet the agreed responsibility. It is wise for parents to remember that children need to be frequently and calmly reminded of their responsibilities and it is up to parents to ensure that children do not slide out of responsibility. It is important that the sanction fits the 'crime' as unjust consequences rarely induce responsible behaviour.

Authoritarian discipline systems tend to stress the 'do nots' demanded within the home. Such an approach does not demonstrate to children what to do and hence does not foster the child's own self-control and responsibility within and outside the home. Furthermore, control by domination or by rigid practices produces children who are either shy and insecure or overbold and insecure, and is certain to produce storms during adolescence.

At the other extreme, there are families where no standards operate, total latitude is allowed and anything goes. Such lack of discipline will produce a child who has never learned much about self-control.

The most destructive form of behavioural management is unpredictable control where the parents shift, in random fashion, from rigid to democratic to no control so that the children do not know what precisely are the limits and responsibilities within and outside the family. Where this system operates, children are not able to develop either security or self-confidence, and their childhood uncertainties will pursue them into adolescence and often into adult life.

Children are much more likely to adhere to their responsibilities when parents themselves model appropriate behavioural control. It is unfair to ask children to do things you do not do yourself. When children fail to meet their responsibilities then sanctions need to be employed to ensure a return to responsible behaviour. However, any breakdown of responsibility on the child's part first needs to be discussed in terms of what led to the irresponsible behaviour. When a legitimate reason (for example, sickness) is evident then no sanction needs to be imposed.

EXAMPLES OF IN-HOME RESPONSIBILITIES FOR SCHOOL-GOING CHILDREN

- ☐ Being on time for meals
- ☐ Rising from bed when called
- ☐ Washing and dressing self
- ☐ Eating food slowly
- ☐ Asking to be excused when rising from meal table
- ☐ Walking in an orderly way around home
- ☐ Doing homework at designated times
- ☐ Communicating in a respectful way with parents and other family members
- ☐ Respecting other people's property
- ☐ Not using other people's belongings without permission
- ☐ Speaking at an acceptable volume
- ☐ Responding positively to requests from parents and other family members
- ☐ When distressed or angry requesting personal time with parents or other family members
- ☐ Playing with other children (or adults!) in a way that is safe
- ☐ Keeping common rooms and own personal space tidy and clean
- ☐ Accepting fairly allocated domestic responsibilities (for example, washing-up after meals, bringing in fuel, putting soiled clothing in laundry basket)

EXAMPLES OF OUT-OF-HOME RESPONSIBILITIES FOR SCHOOL-GOING CHILDREN

- ☐ Being on time for school
- ☐ Attending school as required

- [ ] Being respectful of the property and belongings of the school, teachers, fellow students and secretarial and maintenance staff
- [ ] Carrying out assigned responsibilities within the school and classroom
- [ ] Coming home on time from school
- [ ] Communicating in a respectful fashion with teachers, fellow students and other adults and children
- [ ] Communicating in a positive way any dissatisfactions arising within the school and classroom to class teacher, school principal and parents
- [ ] Playing in a safe way with peers
- [ ] Speaking at an acceptable volume
- [ ] Handing up assigned homework
- [ ] Respecting public property

DEVELOPING CHILDREN'S SELF-CONTROL

There are three essential aspects to the successful development of self-control and responsibility in children:

- sanctions need to be used positively
- parents' words need always to matter
- conflict with children needs to be avoided.

Each of these aspects is discussed in detail below.

The positive use of sanctions

It has already been pointed out that sanctions are employed within the home (as well as in schools and public places) not to punish people but to ensure adherence to agreed responsibilities. Within the home, it is vital that sanctions are employed within a context where:

- parents and other family members have unconditional, positive relationships with each other
- positive, respectful ways of communicating are used
- parents model appropriate responsible behaviours
- effort rather than performance is consistently encouraged.

The implementation of a sanction is best done in such a way that the child knows precisely:

- how he has been irresponsible, and
- what exactly is required of him.

Sanctions are used to educate for responsibility; they are not a means of 'putting down' children. The positive use of sanctions has certain clear characteristics:

1. When possible, the sanction used needs to be the *natural result of the irresponsible behaviour.* For example, if a child is messing with his food, then the natural sanction is to take the food away. If a child in a temper throws building blocks all over the room, a natural sanction is to get him to pick up every piece.
2. Sanctions need to *be predictable and consistent.* This means that children always know where responsibility lies and know that breaching that line will always lead to the application of a sanction. Furthermore, children need to know that no matter which parent (or grandparent, or child-minder) is involved or which child in the family chooses to be irresponsible, the same sanction will occur.
3. Sanctions need to be *fair and just:* the sanction needs to fit the irresponsibility. When sanctions are agreed by the family and not left up to the whim of one member then the possibility of injustice is considerably lessened. Regular reviews of the responsibility system also guard against injustice.

4. Sanctions need to be *impersonal.* The adult who loses her temper with a child who is uncooperative and assigns a sanction that arises from her own projections and neurotic need for order and perfectionism will not be effective with children. The child knows that the sanction is only an outlet for the adult's dependence and frustration, and will blame the adult rather than himself.

5. Sanctions need to *emphasise what is expected* of children so that when they occur they become an opportunity for more responsible behaviour and self-control.

6. Sanctions need to be *withheld* until the adult in charge understands the psychological function of the irresponsible behaviour. She then assigns the sanction in a way that reflects that understanding. (See pp. 149–53 for further elaboration on this point.)

7. Sanctions need to be *positively and calmly applied* so that the child does not become fearful of the adult in charge. Fear blocks communication between child and parent. Furthermore, a child who is frightened may agree to anything but, when he recovers, nothing will have been learned and the next action of irresponsibility may be worse than the first.

8. The *child's first name* needs to be used in assigning a sanction.

What sanctions are available within the family? Different homes demand different solutions and each family needs to determine the best responsibility system for its unique culture. Therefore the list on page 82 is just a general guideline.

Words need always to matter

The hallmarks of an effective system of behavioural control within the family are *predictability*, *specificity* and *consistency*.

SANCTIONS AVAILABLE FOR FAMILIES

- ☐ Positive and firm request for responsible behaviour.
- ☐ Withdrawal of attention from the irresponsible action (this is very often effective, as the ploy can be to get the parent's attention).
- ☐ Deprivation of privileges (the possible loss of a favourite activity can become a strong motivation for responsibility).
- ☐ Detention with a meaningful purpose (this needs to be supervised and the supervisor needs clear directions on what task has been assigned to the child, for example, tidy up the room, complete the wash-up, complete homework).
- ☐ Assignment of domestic responsibility (for example, cut grass, vacuum downstairs rooms).
- ☐ Warning of deprivation of some future privilege (for example, staying overnight with a friend, going to cinema to see new popular release).
- ☐ Deprivation of pocket money.

Predictability means the child knows precisely how you will react to a given behaviour, be it responsible or irresponsible. Predictability applies whether you make a promise or threaten a sanction. Words begin to matter to children when they are carried into action. A parent who promises or threatens but does not follow through will not be successful in developing responsibility and self-control in a child. In this situation, the child does not know where the limits lie, and he will push and push until he finds those limits. Parents often excuse their lack of predictability by such remarks as 'he's only a child', or 'she will learn soon enough' or 'give him one more chance'. If such responses are frequent then the child will not learn self-control.

Parents are best to define specifically their promise or sanction. To promise a child, in response to a responsible action or just as a spontaneous loving gesture, that 'we'll do something nice at the weekend' is too vague and also too easily forgotten. To say 'I will bring you to the cinema on Saturday and you can choose which film you would like to see' is clear and will not be forgotten by the child. Likewise, with regard to a sanction; it is not, for example, specific enough to say 'if I catch you playing out on the main road, I'll kill you'. This is a message most children will ignore because they know full well that you will not kill them. Again your words now cease to matter.

The third hallmark of an effective behavioural management system is consistency of response across situations, persons in charge and individual children. If the two parents operate different responsibility systems, then the children end up confused, because they are not sure which parent to follow. Also, like many adults, children will exploit such a weakness in the system in order to slide out of responsibilities. Every parent knows how children can play off one parent against another, or one teacher against another. There is no point in blaming the child for exploiting such a loophole. The problem lies with those who are responsible for implementing the system of control, and not with the child. Blaming and criticising the child in this situation will generally escalate the problem, lead to a breakdown in communication between parents and child and block self-worth. It is therefore important within a family that the parents have a joint approach on developing responsible behaviour in their children so that they experience a consistent response from both parents.

Again, for the sake of consistency, there cannot be one set of expectations for one child and another for a second child. Parents often have 'favourites' in the family. The problem with this is that the other children in the family will feel less valued and less inclined to respond to demands for responsibility when such demands are not also being made of the 'favourite'. The rebellion of the children who are belittled becomes a means of expressing their anger and feelings of rejection.

Consistency across situations means no matter where the responsible or irresponsible action takes place the parent or adult in charge will respond in the same way. For example, a child throws a temper tantrum at home in order to get sweets before his dinner but his mother does not give in and the temper tantrum is totally ignored. When the child throws a tantrum in the supermarket his mother needs to respond in the same way she did at home. However, some parents give in 'for peace sake' or because they worry 'what will people think of me when they see my child screaming his head off?' You weaken the child's self-control when you respond in this way. Furthermore children are quick to spot a parent's vulnerability and will exploit it for their own ends.

Do not get into conflict with children

When a child is exhibiting difficult, uncooperative or aggressive behaviours, it is important that the parent remains calm, though positively firm. Matters will only escalate if the parent allows herself to be trapped into conflict with the child. When the parent loses control, the child, who is being irresponsible, gains even more control both of the situation and of the parent. The child is also given further licence to engage in the disruptive behaviours. The issue here is that aggression breeds aggression, hostile silences breed hostile withdrawal, and any type of 'put down' responding (cynicism, sarcasm, ridiculing, scolding, etc.) only aggravates the situation. When a parent remains absolutely calm and unflappable in the face of the child's unacceptable behaviours, the child will gain self-control much more speedily. He will see that the behaviour is not gaining the desired outcome and it will extinguish. Sometimes, the child may escalate the distressing behaviour in order to 'break down' the parent's resolve but as long as the parent stays calmly firm in her resolve to remain separate from the child's problematic behaviour then self-control by the child will gradually emerge. When the child is calm it can be made clear that such behaviour is difficult and will not bring him any gain. At the same time, the child can be shown how to ask appropriately for what he wants. It may also be pointed out that not all needs can be met immediately, that some needs are unreasonable and that sometimes resources may not be available to meet needs.

Sometimes, no matter what the parent does, the child persists in the disruptive behaviours. Clearly in such a situation the parent's calm and patience will begin to wear thin. When this happens the best policy is for the parent to remove herself from the child. Losing control will not help one bit.

When a child continues to engage in out-of-control behaviour some immediate action is needed in order to diffuse the situation. Sometimes the best action is no action. Verbally confronting a child who is out of control rarely works (even though the parent may do so in a positive way) as the child is emotionally upset and a request for reasonable behaviour is likely to fall on deaf ears. There is nothing better than hurt, anger or fear to deafen a child to the voice of reason (same for adults!). In this context, emotion is always stronger than reason. The 'no action' response takes the focus off the child and, because the behaviour is not eliciting a response, it can quickly extinguish when no reaction is forthcoming.

If a child's behaviour puts the parent or other children at risk then some decisive action is required. When other children are at risk, the parent needs to quietly and calmly request them to leave the room. It is not wise for the parent to physically approach the child who is troubled but stay at a distance, silent and calm.

If a child physically attacks a parent, it is essential that she does not retaliate as this will only aggravate the situation. She needs to calmly back away from the child and maintain strong eye contact so that the child sees the parent is in control. If this is not possible, then just holding the child's body so that he cannot kick out or use his arms can serve as a protection for both child and adult.

The undercontrol behaviours that most upset parents are: aggressiveness, insolence, screaming and vulgar language. It is wise to be aware that such out-of-control behaviours inevitably arise from the hidden need to be loved, valued and accepted, and are preceded by some experience during which the child felt hurt, angry or frightened. When the child has calmed down, the parent can give him a normal amount of affection and safety, and attempt to discover what had hurt, angered or frightened him. Even though some sanction may still need to be applied, it can be done now within the context of this understanding. Indeed, the parent may find that she needs to change some aspect of her behaviour towards the child.

No matter what the situation is, analysis of the event best takes place afterwards, in a secure and safe setting for both the child and the parent, in order to determine what precipitated the child's behaviour, to see what the child and adult can both learn from the situation and to determine what sanction (if any) needs to be applied.

BEHAVIOURAL CONTROL AND YOUR CHILD'S EDUCATION

Clearly, behavioural control on the part of each member of the family is essential for the resolution of family conflicts. When members are out of control (shouting, hitting, blaming, criticising, being cynical, being sarcastic, ridiculing, scolding) then there is no forum for the resolution of conflict. The absence of such behaviours is a prerequisite for conflict resolution, whether the conflict is between parent and parent, or between parents and child.

It is equally important for the child's educational development that he has learned responsibility and self-control by the time he enters primary school. If a child has not learned basic concentration skills, listening skills, control of voice-level, ability to make requests in an appropriate manner, body control and appetite management (in terms of food and drink), then he is going to find it very difficult to be attentive and responsive within the classroom situation and will probably pile up problems for himself quite quickly. The teacher may get impatient with him and may label him as 'slow', 'hyperactive', 'lazy', 'not too bright' or 'impossible'. These labels (unjustified though they may be) can dog a child's academic path for the rest of his school days. In Chapter 8 on parents as educators, the issue of preparing children for school life is discussed in detail.

KEY INSIGHTS

- ☐ Behavioural control starts with the parents.
- ☐ Parents who lose control of themselves and respond critically to children give children control over them.
- ☐ It is not the parents' job to control children.
- ☐ It is a recipe for conflict to get one person to control another.
- ☐ Sanctions are used to educate for responsibility.
- ☐ Words matter to children when parents predictably and consistently carry them into action.
- ☐ Parents are advised not to get trapped into conflict with children.

KEY ACTIONS

☐ Parents who are troubled in themselves need to seek help so that they do not pass on their problems to their children.

☐ Ensure that members of your family take responsibility for their own self-control.

☐ Educate your children to take responsibility for themselves.

☐ Frequently remind your children of their responsibilities within and outside the home.

☐ Ensure that your children do not slide out of responsibility.

☐ Ask your children to do only what you yourself are willing to do.

☐ Ensure that you and your partner have a consistent and joint approach to developing responsible behaviour in your children.

CHAPTER 5

PARENTS' OWN SELF-ESTEEM

IMPORTANCE OF SELF-ESTEEM OF PARENTS

There are many personal, interpersonal, parental, occupational and career reasons why parents need to understand the nature of self-worth and self-esteem, the development of self-esteem and how to elevate it as an adult. Medical evidence shows a strong association between physical health, happy longevity and high self-esteem. Likewise, psychology and, more recently, dynamic psychiatry, show that people's neurotic and psychotic problems, as well as marital and family problems, are related to personal vulnerability and feelings of inferiority or superiority. Indeed, the well-being of all human systems is largely determined by the level of self-esteem of its participants. When the system has caring, just and supportive structures, it aids the healthy development of each member. But such structures are unlikely to be created by the leaders of the system unless they have high self-esteem.

I have been a member of many different systems during my lifetime – educational, religious, healthcare, industrial, community – and I have remained unimpressed by the level of care, understanding, compassion and support within these systems. Clearly, leaders have a higher responsibility than others to realise their self-worth as low self-esteem leads to ineffective leadership. Parents are the leaders of the family and it is now well established that their individual levels of self-esteem determine the physical, psychological and social well-being of each member of the family. Parents with middle to low self-esteem will effect similar levels of self-esteem in their children and maintain such levels in each other. Conversely, the parent with high self-esteem is the most effective parent.

You have already seen in Chapter 2 how important the self-esteem of the individual partners is to the couple relationship; likewise, the self-esteem of the parents is important to the well-being of the family. All the clinical evidence now suggests that the more independent, separate, secure and personally fulfilled the person is, the more he is able to develop effective couple and family relationships. On the other hand, the more dependent, enmeshed, insecure, and unfulfilled the partner or parent is, the more problems are likely to develop within marriages and families.

You have seen that self-worth is concerned with your feelings about two aspects of yourself – your lovability and your capability. When you walk into a roomful of people, do you automatically feel you are someone worthy of value and respect or do you slide into a room hoping not to appear conspicuous? If the latter applies to you, this signifies that you have a self-esteem screen. When you are asked to do something, do you immediately believe you have the capability to do it, or if you have not, that you can certainly learn, or do you quickly say 'no' or denigrate yourself by saying something like 'you're asking the wrong person'? Again, if the latter applies to you, this signals self-esteem protectors.

Your self-esteem – how you feel about yourself – influences how you feel about every aspect of your life:

- the kind of friends you choose
- how you get along with others
- the kind of person you marry

- your success in your career
- your stability and integrity
- whether you will be a leader or a follower
- your effectiveness as a parent.

Your present sense of self forms the centre of your personality and determines the uses you make of your limitless capacity as a human being. It is not genes which determine your human effectiveness but your self-esteem. The level of self-esteem you emerge with from your childhood determines your level of fulfilment in adult life. However, you are not stuck with the self-esteem legacy from childhood and once you develop awareness of your self-esteem level you can systematically set about changing it, if that is what you want.

By and large people may be described as having one of three levels of self-esteem: low, middle or high. Feeling 'low' is not the same as having low self-esteem. There are many reasons for feeling low in this world – man's inhumanity to man abounds – but the person with high self-esteem who feels low can admit to it, and will often try to do something about the injustices in the world. However, a person with low self-esteem will not admit to vulnerability as this would mean risking rejection. The screen, the front, the face, or the cover-up is the all-important protection for the person with middle to low self-esteem; the lower the person's self-esteem, the more extreme the masks presented to the world.

LEVELS OF ADULT SELF-ESTEEM

Each parent who reads this book has a particular level of self-esteem. Parents with low self-esteem have a deep self-hatred, are highly neglectful of self and are either extremely overdemanding of self or overdemanding of others. Parents with a middle level of self-esteem have serious doubts about their lovability and capability and are highly dependent on the approval of others and on success. Parents with high self-esteem, a very rare breed, most of the time have a deep and quiet acceptance of self and of others.

INDICATORS OF LOW (HIGHLY PROTECTIVE) SELF-ESTEEM

- Highly dependent
- Pessimistic and fatalistic
- No sense of 'good' about self
- Condemning of self
- Extreme perfectionist
- 'Drop-out'
- Extremely fearful of new situations
- Highly critical of all aspects of self
- Believes everybody else is better off
- Deep inferiority complex or superiority complex (which is a cover-up of a sense of inferiority)
- Lonely and isolated
- Unable to form close and deep emotional relationships
- Sees oneself as unlovable
- Sometimes suicidal
- Rigid and inflexible
- Highly blaming of others or total denial of vulnerabilities

- Bottles up feelings or can be dangerously aggressive and violent
- Neglectful of physical welfare
- Rejecting of self
- Possessive of others
- Constant need for reassurance
- Manipulative of others
- Feelings easily hurt
- Highly sensitive to criticism
- Engages in protective communication (for example, hostile silences, sulking, sarcasm, cynicism, blaming, ridiculing)
- Fear change
- Cannot take compliments or positive feedback
- Continually unhappy
- Troubled relationships with others
- Worrier
- Highly prone to anxiety and depression
- Moody

→

- ☐ Feels different from all others
- ☐ Feels guilt about pleasure experiences for self
- ☐ Fears rejection
- ☐ Fearful of mistakes and failure
- ☐ Indecisive
- ☐ Lives life according to rules of 'should', 'should not', 'have to', 'must' and 'ought to'
- ☐ Ashamed of self
- ☐ Feels life is not worth living
- ☐ Displays overinvolvement or underinvolvement in other people's lives
- ☐ Constantly trying to prove self

INDICATORS OF MIDDLE (MODERATELY PROTECTIVE) SELF-ESTEEM

- ☐ Dependent
- ☐ Approval-seeker
- ☐ People-pleaser
- ☐ Difficulties in seeking support, help, advice etc.
- ☐ Cautious and unadventurous
- ☐ Fearful of new situations
- ☐ Can take some criticism
- ☐ Moderate degree of optimism
- ☐ Critical of others' differences
- ☐ Threatened by opposition
- ☐ Expressive of some feelings
- ☐ Conformist
- ☐ Doubts about various aspects of self: physical, intellectual, social etc.
- ☐ Unsure
- ☐ General feeling of dissatisfaction
- ☐ Blaming of others
- ☐ Denial of problems
- ☐ Insecure in relationships
- ☐ Compares oneself with others
- ☐ Jealous of others' success, possessions etc.
- ☐ Critical of self and others
- ☐ Some neglect of physical welfare
- ☐ Aggressive or passive
- ☐ Intolerant of frustration
- ☐ Compliant or rigid
- ☐ Lives in the future
- ☐ Low autonomy
- ☐ Very ambitious
- ☐ Hostile sense of humour
- ☐ Perfectionist
- ☐ Tendencies to worry and anxiety

INDICATORS OF HIGH (MINIMALLY PROTECTIVE) SELF-ESTEEM

- Independent
- Open and spontaneous
- Optimistic, excited and challenged by life
- Flexible
- Engages in direct and clear communication
- Owns own problems, feelings, perceptions, ambitions etc.
- Emotionally close to a few significant others
- Accepting of self and others
- Respects and values others' differences
- Listens to others
- Can take criticism and feedback
- Tolerant of frustrations
- Physically healthy
- Emotionally mature
- Encouraging of self and others
- Realistic awareness of strengths and weaknesses
- Sees weaknesses as opportunities for developing strengths
- Problem-solver
- Expressive of all feelings
- Resistant to conformity
- Seeks support, advice, help, comfort when needed
- Wholehearted involvement in all aspects of life
- Trusts and values self
- Caring of others
- Positively firm with self and others who attempt to impose artificial values
- Cares for environment
- Spiritual
- Needs privacy

ORIGINS OF ADULT SELF-ESTEEM

The development of self-esteem is outlined fully in Chapter 6 on the development of the child's self-esteem. In brief summary, the origins of self-esteem lie primarily in the early experiences of life. Generally, the early relationships with the important adults in our lives (parents, relatives, teachers) are of a mixed nature in terms of being positive and affirming or negative and dismissive. These relationships with important adults are the 'looking glass' for the child and determine the self-image that forms in her mind. The strength of what we see in the looking glass is vividly illustrated in the case of people who are anorexic or bulimic. Relatives and helpers frequently get irritated, frustrated and even aggressive with the person with this high-risk psychosomatic condition. These others, who are concerned, can see that physically the person is wasting away in front of their eyes and cannot understand why she cannot see this as well. The problem is that the internal, hateful self-image of the person, built up in childhood, is much stronger than the image others see of her or that is pointed out in the mirror. Unless her own hidden image of self changes, all the badgering and force-feeding will not effect change in this person, who is so deeply distressed.

Since parents and other significant adults are your mirrors in childhood, if you mostly experienced physical and emotional affection, affirmation, praise, encouragement, support, tenderness, listening, challenge, play, understanding and positive firmness, you will now have a high level of self-esteem. If, on the other hand, you frequently experienced absence of affection or caring that was unfeeling, scolding, ridiculing, critical and physically abusive, or were exposed to hostile silences, unrealistic expectations and standards of behaviour and 'put-down' labels, you will now present an inferior image of yourself. Few of us experience a high proportion of positive experiences and, as a result, there are very few people with high self-esteem. Many people have middle self-esteem and a sizeable number have low to extremely low self-esteem or no sense of self at all. It is now estimated that 85–90 per cent of people need some form of counselling, psychotherapy, psychoanalysis or family therapy in order to correct internal and external blocking behaviours.

MAINTENANCE OF LOW ADULT SELF-ESTEEM AND HIGH PROTECTORS

It is true that your childhood experiences determine your level of self-esteem. However, as an adult you cannot continue to blame the adults who influenced you in your early life for how you feel about yourself now. If you continue to do that, then you will not change. By rejecting the responsibility for how you feel about yourself, you, as an adult, are perpetuating the early negative influences of conditionality or total neglect or other neglectful experiences, and in doing so (whether consciously or subconsciously) you are maintaining or even exacerbating your low level of self-esteem. What then are the behaviours that maintain your poor feelings about self? Some of the most crucial behaviours are listed below and discussed in the following sections.

- rigid and inflexible attitudes about oneself, others, the present and the future
- self-talk of a self-deprecating nature or that is critical and blaming of others and the world
- neglectful and imbalanced lifestyle
- blocking positive experiences
- setting yourself up for rejection
- avoiding challenges
- protective communication patterns
- failure to separate out from parents.

Rigid and inflexible attitudes

Rigid and inflexible attitudes are reflected in the 'shoulds', 'should nots', 'have tos', 'ought tos' and other rigid rules by which adults with self-esteem screens live their lives. Examples are:

- □ 'I should never make a mistake.'
- □ 'I should not let myself down in front of others.'
- □ 'I must not get angry.'
- □ 'Everybody should like me.'
- □ 'Nobody should criticise me.'
- □ 'I ought to stay home with my mother.'
- □ 'I must never say "no" to somebody who needs me.'
- □ 'I must not think of myself.'
- □ 'I should be successful.'
- □ 'I have to be on time.'
- □ 'I have to have everything perfect.'
- □ 'The children must obey me.'
- □ 'Others should see things my way.'
- □ 'This train should be on time.'
- □ 'The bank assistant should be more approachable.'
- □ 'People should work harder.'
- □ 'Things will never change.'
- □ 'You are the way you are.'
- □ 'Some people are just stupid.'

All these examples demonstrate a lack of sensitivity and caring towards oneself. They put unreasonably high demands on yourself and others and, unfortunately, perpetuate your poor opinion of self. If you truly loved and valued yourself and others, you would not treat yourself or others in such a dismissive way. These are the messages you heard in your early life and which you now continue to repeat to yourself. These attitudes also reflect your high dependence on others and on success for good feelings about yourself.

In some cases, the person's attitude goes beyond conditional regard to outright rejection of self. I recall a medical doctor who came for help and who, in his own words, saw himself as a 'lump of shit'. He was very neglectful of himself, had been on anti-depressants for years and could be quite violent towards his wife and children. Not surprisingly, his childhood history was similar to what he was now repeating with his own family. Other clients I have helped described themselves as 'being of no value', 'ugly', 'nothing', 'empty', 'hateful', 'loathsome' or 'dirty'.

Deprecatory self-talk

The way you talk to yourself or think arises from the attitudes you have towards yourself, others and the world. If you have hateful attitudes towards yourself – expressed, for example, in attitudes of 'I'm no good', 'everybody else is better than I am' or 'the world is a cruel place to be' – then the way you think and talk will reflect your self-hatred, as in these examples:

- □ 'Don't ask me to do that, I'd be no good at it.'
- □ 'I dread going into work today.'
- □ 'I'm stupid and useless.'
- □ 'Why am I different from everybody else?'
- □ 'Everybody else seems so confident and happy.'
- □ 'I never do anything right.'
- □ 'I'm not doing that course if I have to do an examination at the end of it.'
- □ 'I'm not going out there to make a fool of myself.'
- □ 'Everybody else on the course will be cleverer than I am.'
- □ 'Nobody could find me attractive.'
- □ 'I always feel miserable and lonely.'
- □ 'Everyone is against me.'
- □ 'I bet they're talking about me.'
- □ 'I'll never get on in this job.'

Because all these messages to yourself are infused with feelings of hate, dislike and rejection of self, they have the same impact on your self-esteem as had the rejecting, dismissive, neglecting messages you heard from parents and others when you were a child. These messages also serve a protective function because they either block you from risk-taking or block others from approaching you. People with low self-esteem keep others at a distance because to let others too close emotionally would be to risk rejection; they might see through the mask to the real person behind it. There is value in listening to your self-talk. If you make a list of your thoughts and your verbal messages to yourself you may find that you are continuing to maintain, or perhaps even further expanding, your low self-esteem.

Unhealthy lifestyle

Self-esteem is revealed in all sorts of ways but how you look after yourself in your everyday life is one major indication of how you feel about yourself. Check the list on page 100 and see how you fare in this regard.

If you engage in one or more of the above behaviours you are showing clear signs of a self-esteem screen. The more you continue such neglectful ways the more you cease to see yourself as worthy of nurture and a balanced, healthy lifestyle, and so the neglectful lifestyle maintains your middle to low self-esteem.

Blocking positive experiences

An adult with low self-esteem will find it very difficult to internalise a compliment or to accept affection or positive feedback. For such a person, the emotional conviction of his own unworthiness is far stronger than any one-off or random positive experience. It is also

CHECKLIST OF BEHAVIOURS INDICATING UNHEALTHY LIFESTYLE

- ☐ Rushing and racing
- ☐ Missing meals
- ☐ Eating on the run
- ☐ Overeating
- ☐ Undereating
- ☐ Dependent on alcohol
- ☐ Dependent on drugs (for example, Tagamet, tranquillisers, sleeping tablets, anti-depressants)
- ☐ Working long hours
- ☐ Frequently late for appointments
- ☐ Trying to do several things at the one time
- ☐ Rarely saying 'no' to demands made of you
- ☐ Having no time for self
- ☐ Few or no social outings
- ☐ Having little or no leisure time
- ☐ Lacking physical exercise
- ☐ Suffering from sleeplessness
- ☐ Overtired
- ☐ Rarely or never asking for help
- ☐ Aggressive towards others
- ☐ Passive in the face of unrealistic demands or abusive behaviours
- ☐ Manipulative
- ☐ Lacking caution (for example, don't wear seat-belt, drive with drink taken, carelessly cross busy thoroughfares)
- ☐ Having little family time
- ☐ Having to do everything perfectly
- ☐ Not taking care of your own or others' belongings
- ☐ Living in the future or in the past
- ☐ Fretful
- ☐ Worrying all the time

too risky for the person with low self-esteem to let in the positive message as the chances of rejection are greater if the other person is allowed to get close. I remember an incident from my own life that highlights this issue of blocking positive messages from others. As a young student, I had an extremely low image of myself, particularly with regard to my physical self. I saw myself as ugly and unattractive, and was convinced that no woman would find me interesting. Because of this, my tendency was to avoid contact with women and I developed the ability to always find a corner to hide in. At one party, to which I had been reluctantly dragged by a well-meaning male friend, I had found my corner but was interrupted by two women who came over to me saying, 'come on out and join us'. Rather than responding positively to their request, I demurred and thought, 'they are only feeling sorry for me; they don't really want to talk to me'. I spent the rest of the evening in the corner. A number of years later, when I was some way on the road to increasing my self-esteem, I met one of the two women. Somehow, I brought up the incident and she was quite amazed because she had gone away from the encounter at the party thinking, 'he obviously doesn't find us interesting'. She had not seen at all that I lacked the confidence to take up their offer, and I had missed the opportunity for a relationship that might have helped me to see myself in a more positive way.

Dismissal of positive messages maintains the person's poor self-esteem but is, unfortunately, quite a common characteristic of many people. Some examples of blocking positive messages are given below:

- □ 'You don't really mean that, do you?'
- □ 'Ah, you're only saying that to please me'.
- □ 'Just a stroke of luck, that's all it was'.
- □ You must be looking for something' (following a compliment).
- □ 'People are just out to fool you'.
- □ 'You don't really know me'.
- □ 'You'll think differently tomorrow'.

Setting yourself up for rejection

One of the saddest aspects of the behaviour of individuals with middle to low self-esteem is that they often set themselves up for rejection. Each person has a need to feel valued and accepted by others and none more so than those who lack a sense of value and acceptance of themselves. They so much want to be loved and approved of, but are frightened of reaching out for such responses. Indeed, the very behaviours they employ to gain recognition almost always result in their being rejected. Typical behaviours used to gain recognition, but which can lead to rejection, include:

- Possessiveness
- Controlling
- Withdrawal
- Sulking
- Constantly looking for reassurance
- Hypersensitivity to criticism
- Aggression
- Passivity
- Perfectionism

The purpose of these behaviours is to gain acceptance; they are not used to hurt other people. Unfortunately, what most often transpires is that the person who is the target of such behaviours eventually rebels (see opposite).

All these reactions confirm the person's worst inner fears – that he is no good, unworthy, weak, despicable or unlovable – and so he is thrown back into feeling bad about himself again.

Why do people use these maladaptive ways to gain acceptance? The simple answer is that the adaptive ways did not work for them as children, whereas the maladaptive behaviours at least partially

BEHAVIOUR	REACTION OF OTHER PERSON
□ Possessiveness	'Get off my back'; 'I can't breathe with your possessiveness'
□ Controlling	'Stop telling me what to do'; 'Just let me do things my own way'
□ Withdrawal	'Stay away'; 'You're just like a child'; 'Don't come back'
□ Sulking	'I can't stand that face you put on'; 'I'm sick and tired of your sulks'
□ Constant need for reassurance	'Will you stop nagging me?'; 'You're driving me crazy with your incessant enquiries'; 'Grow up'
□ Hypersensitivity to criticism	'My God, I can't even say "boo" to you'; 'I'm just going to keep my mouth shut in future'
□ Aggression	'That is the last you'll see of me'; 'You're just a bully and a no-good'
□ Passivity	'I can't live with your martyrdom any more'; 'For goodness sake, will you say something?'; 'You're like a mouse'
□ Perfectionism	'This home is like a clinic'; 'This house is more important than I am'

worked. Every child reaches out adaptively to love and be loved and accepted unconditionally, but when this method fails, a range of maladaptive means develops. Parents and teachers talk of children who are attention-seekers, bullies, easily upset, perfectionist, people-pleasers, disruptive and so on. What needs to be recognised is that these are attempts by children to gain the acceptance they have received imperfectly or not at all.

Avoiding challenges

It is through the challenges in our lives that we grow in knowledge, maturity and self-esteem but change and risk-taking are threatening for people with middle to low self-esteem. Conformity is high on the agenda of such people, and checking out the safety factor before any venture is undertaken is a typical characteristic. Only 10 per cent of elderly people function at a physical, emotional, social, sexual, creative, spiritual and intellectual level that is indistinguishable from younger people. The essential aspect of these elderly people is that they always continued to challenge themselves throughout their lives; they also have high self-esteem. The person with middle to low self-esteem is highly dependent and displays poor initiative and autonomy because the risk of social disapproval is too great to be venturesome. The problem is, however, that as long as you avoid challenges in all, or even some, of the areas of human functioning, you maintain a poor sense of self. Individuals with middle self-esteem tend to take more risks, following a safety check, than those with low self-esteem. Many people who attend courses on awareness and self-development have middle self-esteem whereas the people who need these courses even more are rarely present – again because of the challenges involved. What is equally noticeable is that most men are very slow to attend such courses and can be quite dismissive of psychological and social insights.

Protective communication patterns

Protective patterns of communication, including projection and introjection, have been outlined in Chapter 2. All of these ways of communicating reflect self-esteem vulnerability but also serve to maintain that vulnerability. Protection only maintains helplessness. Furthermore, the person who employs protective communication patterns is rarely assertive regarding needs, since passivity and aggression rarely work as means of getting needs met. The consequence of unfulfilled needs is the reinforcement of feelings of unworthiness. Finally, projection, introjection, aggression, manipulation and passivity eventually alienate the person who is their target, further compounding feelings of unacceptability.

Non-separation from parents

Many adults are still tied to their parents, looking for the unconditional love and affirmation they did not receive or were not permitted to demonstrate as children. It is as if the umbilical cord has not yet been severed. There are many people who, though they are in their twenties, thirties, forties or even fifties, are still living at home. There are others who keep overly frequent contact with parents and often neglect their own marriages and children to attend to parents who are not at all helpless. Many of these adults rationalise that their parents cannot do without them, whereas the real hidden issue is that they cannot do without their parents. They have not yet become separate from their parents and they retain a child–parent relationship rather than developing an adult–adult relationship with their parents. The insecurity of these adults is deep-seated but it will never be resolved through their continuing dependent relationship on parents. Sometimes, people who are insecure may leave home and may even emigrate to faraway places but the umbilical cord remains uncut and they simply transfer their dependence onto others by constantly needing to impress and to be recognised and accepted by others. As long as this dependence on others is maintained their level of self-esteem will continue on a downward slide.

ACTION IS THE KEY TO CHANGING SELF-ESTEEM

Action is the means through which an adult's self-esteem is changed. However, it is equally true to say that you cannot earn worth through what you do. This is paradoxical but then so is much of human behaviour. The issue here is that self-worth is a given, whereas self-esteem develops in response to how parents and others relate to children. If you believe that what you have achieved or the professional status you have attained or the material possessions you have acquired or the public notoriety you have gained or the number of children you have reared or the good deeds you have done make you important and acceptable, then you are highly dependent and vulnerable in terms of self-esteem. Recall that behaviour in any shape or form does not determine your worth as a human being. Behaviour or action is your means of experiencing this world and neither adds to nor detracts from your unique humanity or worth. In the same vein, all actions have a function: failure and mistakes are means to further learning and growth but are not statements about worth.

So, if actions add nothing to your sense of self, what then do I mean by action is the key? From the moment of birth you are a unique phenomenon in this universe that will never be repeated. You are perfect in your being, a one-off happening. Your capability is limitless. Self-worth is like the sun and just as the sun is always there but can become clouded out by 'deep depressions' so too the individual is always of worth, but this sense of self-worth can be clouded out by punishing and rejecting behaviours in the early years of life and the continuing reinforcement of that dark process in later childhood, adolescence and adulthood. The greater the frequency, intensity and extent of these neglectful experiences, the more distant the person is from a sense of his wondrous being.

The person with middle self-esteem will have had a mixture of positive and neglectful experiences, the person with low or very low self-esteem will have had predominantly punishing experiences,

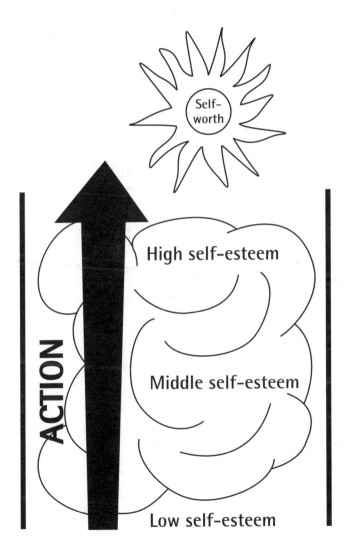

while the person with high self-esteem will have had mostly positive relationships. The person with high self-esteem is very close to his sense of worth, the person with middle self-esteem gets glimpses of his worth through the clouds of doubts and dependence on others, and the person with low or no sense of self rarely, if ever, gets any sightings of the light of his own unique being.

The action needed to increase your self-esteem as an adult is not anything that adds to your self-worth – which is ever present and there since birth – but is the means through which you undo the neglectful experiences of the present and past, and substitute those with unconditional caring behaviours. The action brings you from the dark place of your present level of self-esteem to the place of light, which is a sense of your self-worth. What then are those actions that will bring you along the path to discovering your ever present worth as a human being? In many ways they are the reverse of the actions described above that maintain low levels of self-esteem:

- developing awareness
- positive self-talk
- having a positive relationship with self
- having a healthy lifestyle
- openness to challenge
- engaging in open and relating communication
- letting go of projection and introjection.

Developing awareness

Unless you are aware of what self-esteem is, how it develops and how you may consciously or subconsciously be maintaining a low level yourself, then you are not in a place of readiness to change your level of self-esteem. Awareness is the first step on the path to change, but awareness in itself is not sufficient. Nevertheless, it is important that you continue to develop your awareness of the whole area of self-worth and self-esteem through reading, discussion, seminars, and, when needed, therapy. Action, based on the insights or enlightenment you have acquired, is the essential follow-on step from awareness.

Positive self-talk

Many therapies and self-help books focus on changing the way you think. Their basic premise is that your thinking determines how you feel. For example, if you have fearful, depressive, critical or resentful thoughts then you will feel anxious, depressed, lacking in confidence and resentful. The aim of these therapies is to get you to become aware of your negative thinking patterns and, having identified them, to begin to substitute the negative with positive thought patterns. The difficulty with this approach is that the therapist or book starts out by criticising you for thinking in these faulty ways. They see no purpose to these 'negative thought patterns'. I believe, however, that these thought patterns provide an extremely useful protection against a deep underlying insecurity and a consequent fear of rejection. These emotional vulnerabilities precede the thought patterns. The head protects the heart; it is not the head that creates the emotional difficulties. It has already been shown how thought patterns protect you from criticism, hurt and rejection. However, there is a further point to be made regarding positive thinking. Some therapists believe it is thoughts that change you and, if you regularly practise positive affirmations, you will eventually begin to feel good. All the words in the world will not change you unless they are infused with emotion. For example, to praise Johnny in an off-hand way, 'Johnny, you're a great lad', will not make much impression on Johnny but to say sincerely and genuinely that you are impressed by his efforts will have a lasting effect. It is not the words that Johnny picks up but the feelings in the words. I am not advocating that you stop practising positive thinking but I am suggesting that unless these positive thoughts come from your gut, they will not have a great effect on your self-esteem.

Below is an affirmation exercise which, if regularly practised with deep and sincere feelings, can be very valuable in raising your level of self-esteem.

DECLARATION OF MY UNIQUENESS

- I wonder at my unique being.
- I am a once-off happening in this universe that will never reoccur.
- I love, value, celebrate and own everything about me.
- I love and care for my body which carries every aspect of me. I will nurture, exercise, rest and accept every aspect of my body. I do not want my body to be like anybody else's.
- I love, value and wonder at the limitless capacity of my mind.
- I own my mistakes and failures and realise these do not in any way take from my wondrous capacity. I see mistakes and failures purely as opportunities for further learning.
- I enjoy my achievements and successes but do not hold on to any of them as indicators of my worth. My worth and value are independent of all my actions.
- I strongly distinguish between my being and my behaviour.
- I am unconditional in my regard for myself and others.
- No action on the part of myself or others takes away from my worth, value and uniqueness.
- I own and take responsibility for all my thoughts, images, ambitions, words and actions, whether they be of a positive or

$\longrightarrow$

neglectful nature and whether they be towards others or myself.

□ There are many things I have done or may do that I regret or will regret but I am determined to grow from these experiences and learn to love myself and others more deeply every day.

□ I will be honest and open about behaviour that is distressful to me but in a way that does not put the other person down.

□ Equally, I will be open and listen to what others have to say to me about what behaviours of mine they find distressful and I will take responsibility for any neglect or hurt I may have caused.

□ No matter what happens I will not cease to care for myself or others.

□ I know I have immense abilities to grow and develop in this world. I can touch, see, feel, hear, think, imagine, say and do. I can be deeply close to others. I can be productive. I can make sense and meaning of what often seems an uncaring and cruel world.

□ I will always remain true to my uniqueness and not allow others to impose artificial goals upon me.

□ I am unique, perfect in my being and, once I remain in possession of my wondrous being, I can create a better world for me and others.

Relationship with self

If positive self-talk is not the complete answer to self-esteem protectors, what then is needed to heal inner turmoil? The solution to any problem lies in the causes; when you know those you have the remedy. From earlier chapters describing the effects of the couple and family relationships on the self-esteem of the child it is clear that the causes of low self-esteem lie in those early relationships. If, then, relationships are the cause of self-esteem protectors, the 'cure' must also be a relationship. However, for an adult, a relationship with another person cannot be the means for changing self-esteem. If you rely on another to make you feel good about yourself, then you are dependent on that person, and you are vulnerable and at risk of loss of self-worth should that person leave your life. Acceptance and approval from another do not form a solid foundation for self-worth.

Realising your self-worth can only come about through another kind of relationship which is an intense, enduring, loving, accepting and affirming relationship with yourself. The adult with self-esteem protectors needs to become the unconditionally loving parent to himself that his parents were unable to be because of their own self-esteem screens. When I suggest to people that the most important agent for change is to love yourself, the inevitable reply is: 'How do I do that?' This is not surprising as there is no emphasis within families, schools, the church or other social systems on the development of a relationship with oneself. Instead, dependence on others is fostered with blocking effects on self-worth. The best way to see how you might build up a relationship with yourself is to ask yourself, 'what are the everyday actions I would do for my own child to ensure that I give her a strong and positive sense and love of self?' – and then apply your answers to yourself.

The typical responses people give to this question are:

- □ Love unconditionally
- □ Accept
- □ Hold
- □ Hug
- □ Nurture
- □ Value
- □ Praise efforts

- ☐ Affirm unique aspects
- ☐ Listen
- ☐ Understand
- ☐ Give time to
- ☐ Share
- ☐ Be involved in her life
- ☐ Challenge
- ☐ Encourage
- ☐ Talk positively to
- ☐ Treat
- ☐ Support
- ☐ Be humorous
- ☐ Be positively firm in the face of unacceptable behaviours
- ☐ Advise on request
- ☐ Protect
- ☐ Ensure responsible behaviour
- ☐ Be compassionate
- ☐ Forgive
- ☐ Allow expression of all feelings
- ☐ Believe in child's capability
- ☐ Be fair
- ☐ Be kind

If a child regularly experiences these actions then she will emerge from childhood with high self-esteem. The relationship that an adult needs to have with himself involves the same range of actions. Your relationship with yourself needs to have all the characteristics that a loving and affirming parent–child relationship would have. This relationship needs to be primarily emotional in nature so that all your thoughts and actions towards yourself are infused with a valuing and celebration of self. Love, acceptance and affirmation need to be the experience of every moment in your daily life so that the tide of valuing actions washes out the old actions of rejection of self, conditionality, protective thinking, avoidance of challenge, aggression or passivity, and neglect of physical well-being.

Change occurs by ensuring that all actions are of a self-valuing and caring nature, whether they have to do with rest, hygiene, job, diet, leisure, physical exercise, lifestyle and so on. Some examples are given below:

- Value and unconditionally love yourself and others
- Do things in a calm and relaxed way
- Eat healthy foods
- Give yourself adequate time to eat and digest
- Listen to yourself
- Encourage yourself to do your best
- See mistakes and failures as opportunities for learning
- Be assertive about your own opinions
- Be spontaneous and open
- Follow your own ideas, beliefs and convictions
- Be honest
- Be accepting of self
- Do not accept artificial goals that others may attempt to impose on you
- Be responsive to your own needs and to the reasonable needs of others
- Be moderate in food and drink intake
- Take time and space for yourself
- Take regular physical exercise
- Ensure you have a balanced lifestyle
- Treat yourself
- Challenge yourself

Changing your relationship with yourself is an endless process that needs to be consistently worked on at all times. The old rejecting and dependent ways are likely to be strongly ingrained and it is only through persistent practise of accepting and valuing behaviours that the old protective ways will be eliminated. The rewards of change are high: security, independence, freedom to be yourself, spontaneity, unconditionality with yourself and others, direct and clear communication, peacefulness and tranquillity, openness to change, to others and to life, and increased potential for self-fulfilment.

Healthy lifestyle

Inevitably, adults with poor self-esteem are neglectful of many of their essential needs. It requires considerable discipline to correct this imbalance in lifestyle and to respond to the many different need areas in our lives. The best approach is through simple time-management so that you ensure that at least most of your essential needs are met within any one couple of days. Check the list on page 117 to see how well and how often you meet the needs noted.

Responding to these needs in a regular and active way is a major aspect of the unconditional relationship with yourself that is needed to elevate your self-esteem. Neglect of that responsibility only serves to further weaken your value and sense of yourself.

Challenge

A love of life is a strong indicator of high self-esteem. The person with middle to low self-esteem avoids challenge as the risk of failure is too threatening. Challenges come in all shapes and forms:

- New job
- Further educational courses
- New friendships

- □ Different career
- □ Travel
- □ Alternative reading
- □ New leisure pursuits
- □ Sexual experimentation
- □ Experimentation with decor
- □ Innovations at work
- □ New hobbies
- □ Development of new skills
- □ Listening to different types of music
- □ Joining a self-development group
- □ Asking for a salary rise
- □ Saying 'no'
- □ Expressing your needs
- □ Voicing your own opinions
- □ Listening to people who differ from you

When you take on challenges, you begin to get in touch with the power within you to take responsibility for your own life. Avoidance of change, though protecting you from hurt and humiliation, keeps your self-esteem at a low level.

Open and relating communication

Communication has been dealt with in detail in earlier sections of this book (pp. 38–46, 58–71). Suffice it to say here that when you engage in direct, open and clear communication, the message you give is that you believe you (and the person with whom you are communicating) are worthy of expressing who you are, what your beliefs are and what your needs are. Such communication serves to elevate your self-esteem and your sense of your uniqueness and specialness.

CHECKLIST OF NEEDS

- Emotional needs of love, affection, warmth, closeness, support, understanding, compassion, humour.
- Cognitive needs of intellectual stimulation, challenge, responsibility.
- Behavioural needs for the development of a whole range of skills, for example, cooking, painting, writing, car maintenance, gardening, woodwork.
- Social needs of friendship, companionship, sharing of expertise and knowledge.
- Physical needs of health, fitness, comfort, safety, food and warmth.
- Sensual needs so that the five senses receive adequate stimulation.
- Occupational needs of meaningful work, fair salary, good conditions, recognition for input, benefit systems, promotional opportunities.
- Sexual needs for gratification of sexual drive within the context of a mature and loving relationship.
- Recreational needs of rest, games, sports, hobbies, interests.
- Spiritual needs of transcendence, mystical experiences and meaningful explanation for existence.

Learning from introjection and projection

You have seen that projection and introjection are protective behaviours guarding against hurt and rejection (pp. 19–26). These behaviours are also indicators of deep dependence on others. However, the more you develop your relationship with yourself and become a good parent to yourself, the more you will be able to reduce your dependence on others, extinguish fears of rejection and become separate from parents and others. When that happens, the use of introjection and projection as protective patterns will automatically cease. The process of self-esteem change is a long one and, in the meantime, it is useful to begin to let go of the need to protect yourself, to work on being separate from others and to learn to be always there for yourself.

Like any other process of change, awareness and action are the key elements. Recognising the tendency to introject, to personalise another's behaviour as saying something about you, is the first step to changing that misinterpretation. The second step is the awareness that no matter what another person says or does it is a statement about that person. The first internal action to take when, for example, a person sends you a 'you' message, like 'you're a fool', is to ask yourself quickly, 'what is this saying about the person addressing me?', and then return the message to him in order to get to the hidden 'I' message. In the present example the best way to return the 'you' message is to say, 'in what way do you think I'm a fool?' The answer might be another 'you' message, like 'you just are'. Once again, you calmly return the message: 'but I'm not clear in what way you find me foolish'. A possible retort now is, 'you never consult me on issues'. You are now getting closer to the real hidden message and so you say: 'on what issues would you like me to consult you?' Because you have managed to keep communication open, the 'I' messages may now begin to emerge, such as: 'I never feel included on decisions about the house' or 'I feel you always dismiss my opinions on issues relating to the children' or 'I feel I don't count in your eyes'.

What is clear now is that the original 'you' message (projection by the other person) had hidden 'I' messages about blocked needs. If you had personalised (introjected) the message and had either withdrawn or attacked back, communication would have broken down, the relationship would have suffered and both people would have gone away hurt and bruised. The blocked needs would have remained unmet. At least, when needs are expressed there is an opportunity to explore whether you are in a position to meet them. If the needs are reasonable, then a 'yes' response is generally in order, if the needs are unreasonable, then a 'no' is in order, if the needs are somewhat difficult to meet then negotiation may be necessary. What is important is that all the time you have held on to your own value in yourself and have stayed separate but caring in your response to the other person's communications.

STEPS TO REDUCING INTROJECTION

1. Awareness of tendency to personalise.

2. Awareness that no matter what the other person says or how he sounds or looks at you, the communication is entirely about him and not about you.

3. Internal thought response: 'what's this saying about the person addressing me?'

4. Return message to sender in order to discover the hidden 'I' message.

5. Hold on to your value and acceptance of self.

6. Respond appropriately to revealed blocked needs.

7. Affirm your need to keep communication open at all times.

As with introjection, it is necessary to learn from projection or the shifting of responsibility for yourself onto others. The initial steps are similar to those for changing introjection: awareness of tendency to project, and awareness that all behaviour coming from you is about you, that others are not responsible for you. The first internal action is owning your behaviour and every aspect of you as yours. When you project you put the responsibility for your life onto another. For example, if you say, 'you're impossible to live with' or 'you never listen' or 'you only think about yourself', you are giving a lot of power over to the person you are addressing and you are abrogating your own responsibility for your own needs. In communicating with another, you need to first own your needs and then send an 'I' message about the need you have. Taking the examples just given, you might say: 'I find it difficult to be close to you when you are constantly complaining' or 'I do not feel you listen when I express my needs' or 'I need you to consider my needs and opinions as well as your own'. Having expressed your need, the next step is to accept that your message is not a command but a request; therefore it is best to allow the other person the right to say 'yes' or 'no' to your need without either response affecting your value and respect for the other person or for yourself.

STEPS TO OVERCOMING PROJECTION

1. Recognition of tendency to use projection as a means of getting your needs met.
2. Awareness that projection is a mirror of your dependence on others.
3. Own everything about yourself.
4. Send an 'I' message regarding an unmet need.
5. Allow the person addressed the freedom to say 'yes' or 'no' to an expressed need (whether reasonable, unreasonable or difficult).
6. Take responsibility for getting your own needs met.

When you first begin to work on being more positive and independent in your communication with others, you may feel that you fail more often than succeed. Persist and the gains will be a more valuing relationship with yourself and others. Remember too that the more you elevate your own self-esteem as an individual, the more you will effect a similar level of self-esteem in your children with positive effects on their all-round development, including their educational development.

KEY INSIGHTS

- ☐ The well-being of all social systems is largely determined by the level of self-esteem of the participants.
- ☐ Parents' levels of self-esteem determine the physical, psychological, social and educational well-being of each member of the family.
- ☐ It is not genes which determine your human effectiveness but your self-esteem.
- ☐ Parents who are highly protective (low self-esteem) have a deep self-hatred, are highly neglectful of self and are either extremely overdemanding of self or overdemanding of others.
- ☐ Your childhood experiences determine your level of self-esteem.
- ☐ When people have middle to low self-esteem they engage in a range of behaviours that protect them from any further hurt, humiliation and rejection.
- ☐ You cannot earn worth through what you do.
- ☐ Behaviour or action is your means of experiencing this world and neither adds to nor detracts from your unique humanity or worth.
- ☐ Awareness is the first step on the path to changing your self-esteem; action is the second step.
- ☐ Acceptance and approval from another do not form a solid foundation for an adult's self-esteem.
- ☐ Changing your relationship with yourself is an ongoing process that needs to be consistently worked on at all times.
- ☐ The more you elevate your own self-esteem, the more you will effect a similar level of self-esteem in your children with positive effects on their all-round development, including educational development.

KEY ACTIONS

- ☐ Determine your level of self-esteem.
- ☐ Develop your awareness of the whole area of self-worth and self-esteem and their influences on yourself, your partner and your children.
- ☐ Engage in emotionally infused positive self-talk.
- ☐ Frequently read the 'Declaration of my uniqueness'.
- ☐ Become the unconditionally loving parent to yourself that your parents were unable to be because of their own self-esteem protectors.
- ☐ Develop a relationship with yourself that has all the characteristics of a loving and affirming parent–child relationship.
- ☐ Develop a healthy, balanced lifestyle.
- ☐ Challenge yourself.
- ☐ Learn from introjection and projection as means of protective communication.

CHAPTER 6

YOUR CHILD'S SELF-WORTH AND SELF-ESTEEM

THE CHILD'S SELF-ESTEEM AND EDUCATIONAL EFFORT

You have seen that children's self-esteem is affected by their parents' relationship with each other, by the type of loving shown in the family, by the self-esteem of each of the parents, by teachers' interactions with them and by the way that relatives and other significant adults relate to them. You have also seen that being a member of a subculture may influence self-esteem. The child's level of self-esteem will determine not only his educational progress but also emotional, social, intellectual, sexual, career and spiritual development. In terms of their academic growth, children with high self-esteem are characterised by:

- Retention of natural curiosity
- Eagerness to learn
- Love of challenge
- Ability to focus on the here and now
- Acceptance of failure and mistakes as opportunities for learning
- Tolerance of criticism
- Competitiveness with self not with others
- Acknowledgment of strengths and weaknesses
- Enjoyment of academic effort

- Positive receptivity to reasonable demands and sanctions for irresponsible actions

On the other hand, children with middle to low self-esteem present a very different profile in terms of their educational efforts:

- Loss of natural curiosity
- Fear of failure and mistakes
- Use of avoidance strategies (apathy, low motivation, poor or no application to studies, non-listening, playing truant, day-dreaming)
- Use of compensation strategies (perfectionism, academic intensity, long hours of study or boastful manner but with no academic effort)
- Hypersensitivity to criticism
- 'Teacher-pleasing' or rebelliousness
- Shyness, emotional withdrawal or disruptive behaviour, loud-ness, destructiveness, bullying
- Avoidance of challenge
- Competitiveness or 'couldn't care less' attitude
- Manifestation of self-fulfilling prophecies of failure and rejection
- Self-labelling, for example 'I'm no good at reading', 'I'm hopeless at mathematics', 'I'm useless at sports'
- Open hostility or silent resentment to correction or reasonable demands for more responsible effort
- Overinvolvement in sports activities

If your child displays any of these signs then he has a self-esteem screen, and unless you, as the parent, pay attention to the mirroring of his self-worth, the child is likely either to fail to make academic progress or to break under the strain of having to constantly prove himself academically to you.

There are very specific interactions that parents and other significant adults need to develop in their relationship with children in order for them to feel good about themselves. The emergence of a child's self-worth lies primarily in the hands of parents. Parents act as the mirror for their children and their responses will determine how much of their unique selves children will show. In this regard, there can be no such thing as benign neglect. The child is completely dependent on the parents and, whether parents realise it or not, their every action towards the child affects his realisation of self.

MIRRORING A CHILD'S SELF-WORTH

It is useful to look at a child's sense of self under six main headings:

- the physical aspect (appearance, size, shape, eye colour, hair colour)
- the emotional aspect (whether one is lovable, attractive, interesting)
- the intellectual aspect (whether one is clever, 'bright', has the ability to comprehend certain aspects of the world)
- the behavioural aspect (whether one is skilled, able, independent, noticeable)
- the social aspect (a sense of uniqueness or inferiority or superiority or invisibility)
- the creative aspect (whether one conforms or resists conformity, whether one likes to be the same as or different from others, whether one 'people-pleases' or sees and does things one's own way).

The relationships that parents and other significant adults have with children need to communicate messages in regard to these six aspects of self that engender in the children a deep and genuine celebration of themselves. Sadly, the messages children more typically receive are ones which undermine, weaken, distort, or even destroy any good sense of self. The following sections examine the kind of messages children need to receive in order to maintain self-worth and the kind of messages that lead to middle, poor or no sense of self.

The physical aspect of self

The message that needs to be communicated to children about their bodies is:

Your body is always right.

When they walk into a social setting many adults sidle in, slip in, take a back seat, keep their eyes cast down or give only fleeting glances – all of which behaviours reveal doubts about the physical image. It is a very common insecurity in people to doubt their physical attractiveness. All these doubts come from messages received in early childhood. You are certainly un- likely to have heard that your body is always right, good, unique and beautiful, and need not be like anyone else's body.

What do I mean by 'your body is always right'? The following examples will clarify what is meant. I once saw a four-year-old boy who was frequently bedwetting (enuresis). Enuresis can be either primary or secondary: in the former case the child has never learned how to control the bladder and the causes of the problem may be organic or may be due to poor toilet-training, while in the latter case the child had at one time learned to control the bladder but has lost that ability. The causes of secondary enuresis are nearly always psychological or social. When a parent brings me a child who is manifesting physical symptoms, my first question to myself always is: 'what is this symptom saying that is right about the child?' In the case of the four-year-old boy, I explored his relationship with his mother and, apart from her giving out to him about the bedwetting, the relationship seemed caring and loving. I then explored the child's relationship with his father and found it to be virtually non-existent. The child's father was overambitious, totally involved in his work and neglectful of both his marital relationship and his relationship with his son. Clearly, this man had a self-esteem screen and was busily compensating for his poor view of himself with unfortunate consequences for himself and his child. He usually got home late at night when the child was already in bed. On weekends he tended to go to the office on Saturday and to bring home work to be completed. He spent little or no quality time with his son. I had two hypotheses regarding the 'rightness' of the child's body symptom of bedwetting. First, the symptoms symbolised a concern on the child's part for the mother who was being neglected by her spouse. Any risk of his mother becoming disabled would be a great threat to this child as she was the one on whom he totally depended. Second, the child was feeling rejected by his father and was expressing this loss through his bladder. I decided to act on the latter hypothesis and requested the father to pay a lot more attention to his son, suggesting that when he came home at night, he would go up to the child's room and, whether or not the child was asleep, give him a hug. I also asked that he spend at least thirty undistracted minutes on Saturdays and Sundays with his son. Within two weeks the bedwetting stopped.

A more dramatic case brings home even more clearly how the child's body is always right. It involved a seven-year-old boy who was sent to me with loss of near-sight (his long-sight was perfect) and regular soiling (encompresis). Like enuresis, encompresis can be primary or secondary. In the boy's case it was secondary. Again I asked myself two questions: what is the soiling saying that is right about the child (the soiling preceded the loss of sight)?; what is the loss of near-sight saying that is right about the child?

I discovered that the child was from a broken home: the father had left three years before and had maintained no contact with his son. The child's mother was considerably stressed, had low self-esteem and was trying to hold down a job. She was very irritable with the child and was extremely punishing of his soiling behaviour. One day when he soiled she lost control and smeared the faeces onto his face, into his mouth and into his eyes, and brought him before a mirror, aggressively saying: 'Now look at yourself you little shit-face'. He lost his near-sight immediately after this incident. No organic basis could be found for either the soiling or the loss of sight. Given that the parent is the mirror in which children see themselves, how could this child ever again look closely at himself when his mother saw him as a 'shit-face'? It seemed to me that what the soiling was saying that was right about the child was 'nobody gives a shit about me' (a common symbolic statement of neglect in our culture). Given the mother's irritability and violence and the father's desertion of his son the 'rightness' of the soiling made sense. The loss of sight made even more sense when seen as saying symbolically that 'everyone is blind to my needs' or 'nobody sees me' or 'who would want to look at me?' Through therapy this overwrought mother began to feel better about herself, to establish a more supportive network for herself and to develop more effective parenting skills. Gradually, the relationship between her and the boy improved. The soiling symptom ceased within a couple of months and approximately a year later the child's near-sight began to return.

In what other ways do parents and other adults unwittingly affect the physical self-esteem of children? Frederic LeBoyeur, a French obstetrician, was very concerned about the circumstances under which babies were born. It is likely that most of you who read this book were born into brightly lit rooms and, when the umbilical cord was cut, you were hung upside down and slapped on the bottom. What a first blow to your physical integrity and rightness! You had come from a perfect place that was warm, comfortable and dim, and where all your needs were met, and suddenly you were shunted down a channel and emerged to an onslaught of physical abuse. LeBoyeur believed that babies needed to be born into situations that resembled, as far as possible, the environment of the womb. He suggested that the maternity room needed to be warm, comfortable and dimly lit and that when the baby emerged from the vagina, he should be put across the tummy of the mother before the umbilical cord is cut. In LeBoyeur's system the mother is encouraged to gently massage her baby and it is only during that caring process that the umbilical cord is cut. In this system the physical rightness of the child is being respected. Most of LeBoyeur's ideas have now been adopted by modern maternity hospitals.

Forced feeding is another way in which the child's physical rightness is lessened. In this case the parents' intentions may be good but the means are inappropriate. A child will eat when hungry. You know yourself when you do or do not feel like eating. You also know your resistance and annoyance when somebody tries to force food on you. The parent cannot know when the child is hungry; only the child knows this. Nevertheless, some kitchen tables can become battle-grounds between the child and the parent with the child being shouted at to eat the food before him. A familiar phrase is 'you'll sit at that table and you won't move until you have eaten the last bit of food on your plate'. Some parents resort to cajoling, manipulation, bribery or threats in order to get a child to eat. All of these approaches affect children's physical self-worth as they begin to doubt the rightness of their body signals.

It is the responsibility of parents to put food on the table for children; it is not their responsibility to make the children eat it. Children will eat when they are hungry. When it is clear that the child is not hungry then remove the food plate, let the child know that it is okay not to be hungry and inform him of the time of the next meal. The child may come between meals looking for food but it is not wise to respond as you will find too many demands being made of you. You are not telling children that their bodies are wrong when they look for food between meals but you are saying that, at that particular time, you are unable to respond to their need but you will do so at the next mealtime. Parents tend to worry too much about the child's food intake. Clearly, if a child is persistently not eating a balanced diet then it is always wise to get the child physically checked out. However, a child who is not eating regularly may also be manifesting psychological or social problems.

I recall the case of a three-year-old child who was persistently not eating. No organic reason for her loss of appetite could be found. Both parents came with the child to see me. I observed that the child's father was slim, trim and perfectly groomed. It emerged that he had many insecure feelings regarding his physical self and was compensating for this insecurity through excessive fitness exercises and through spending much time on grooming himself. The cosmetic industry trades on people's doubts about their physical appearance. In more recent times cosmetic surgery has become a thriving business. When a child witnesses a parent being overly meticulous about physical appearance, not daring to go out of the house without resort to the appropriate wardrobe, cosmetics and mirror, the child will come to believe that the body is never right and that there is always something to be done to it before it is deemed acceptable and attractive. In the case of the three-year-old girl who was not eating, the father took his physical insecurity a little further than most parents. He used to tease his daughter about her little fat belly (which all three-year-old children tend to have); calling her 'fatty, fatty, fatty', while pointing to her tummy, was a regular interaction with his child. Children are very intuitive and this child picked up the hidden discomfort of her father with her body shape. His stomach was flat and muscular. She was starving herself in order to lose her fat tummy and gain the acceptance of her father. Correction of the father's conditional interactions with the child and his realisation of his dependence on 'looking right' eventually led to the return of the child to healthy eating.

Forced toilet-training is another way in which a blow may be dealt to the child's physical rightness. Many children learn some variation on the message 'you'll sit on that potty and you won't move until you do something'. In the orphanages of years past, young children used to be tied down on potties and would not be released until they had urinated or defecated. Much worse invasion of their physical integrity was perpetrated by carers who put their fingers up the child's posterior to release the sphincter. Children will learn to control the bladder and sphincter with encouragement and praise, whereas forcing them only serves to distort their image of their bodies. A young mother brought me a four-year-old boy who was holding faeces for weeks on end. Again, and wisely, all necessary medical examinations were carried out but all proved negative. During the first interview with the mother and child, I noticed that every time her son moved she pulled him back. Any movement on his part to explore my office or what was on my desk was blocked and he was made to sit still. A child needs the freedom to explore his environment so that he may learn about and feel secure in that setting. I hypothesised that this mother overcontrolled her son but the one bit of power he could hold on to, and which she could not take from him, was when he defecated. Children typically are given so little power in families that they will inevitably try to find some semblance of power through some behavioural strategy. The mother's overcontrolling was a reflection of her own poor self-esteem and her fear of being a 'bad' mother. When she learned to relax her control of the child, allowed him more freedom to explore and regularly presented him with new challenges, normal defecation returned within a very short space of time.

The physical height of the child also needs to be respected. Adults tend to 'talk down' to children rather than stooping down to their eye level and then communicating. Furthermore, young children love the challenge of doing things for themselves: tying their own buttons, washing their own cups, dressing themselves, washing themselves and so on. As far as conveniently possible, it is important to allow them that right over their own physical selves.

Corporal punishment is yet another action that undermines the child's physical rightness. Many adults still justify the use of physical punishment and yet when you ask them how they would feel if they were to be slapped by someone, because they did not see things their way, the answers range from outraged and angry to embarrassed or humiliated. As an adult, you are likely to be quite well aware that nobody has the right to impinge on your physical integrity. But, just because you are older and bigger than a child does not make your person any more valuable than a child's, nor does your adult status give you more rights. If you do not believe this, then you are operating double standards for adults and children which is very confusing for children. Children do not understand why, if you clipped them across the ear five minutes ago, they cannot use a similar punishing action when you fail to meet their needs. The reprimand 'how dare you hit your Daddy?' is puzzling to a child whose father regularly employs physical means of control. Remember too that aggression breeds aggression and, as a parent, you do not want to teach your children violence or verbal aggression as means of getting their needs met. Generally, when adults use physical punishment as a means of controlling children it reflects their own self-esteem protectors and their lack of knowledge of more constructive ways of developing responsible behaviour in children.

The worst breach of a child's physical integrity is sexual violation. I have worked with many adults who as children experienced such invasion of their physical privacy, and inevitably they had concluded that their bodies were 'bad', 'dirty', 'evil' and so on. As children, it was not safe for them to see that the problem lay with the person who had violated them. Children always blame themselves. Often these children, as adults, either cannot form close physical relations with another (avoidance strategy) or become promiscuous (compensation strategy). Either strategy reveals their hatred and rejection of their bodies. Considerable healing is needed to correct the abuse that has been perpetrated on them.

There are many other ways in which children's physical self-worth can be neglected: remarks about physical size or shape, negative comparisons with others, overfussiness with regard to how they are dressed, overreaction when they mess up their 'perfect little suit' and so on. I remember as a child feeling ugly and unattractive because aunts and uncles always wanted to take my twin brother out but never me. One aunt really put the tin hat on it. I was six years of age when she said: 'maybe, someday you'll be good looking'! By contrast my brother's 'good looks' were always being celebrated. For many years after I hated my physical self and was unable to take the risk of asking any woman for a date. I tended to hide away in corners in social situations (avoidance strategy). It took me a long time to resolve this self-hatred, but now I am closer to accepting my physical self for its uniqueness and I no longer have the desire for my body to be like someone else's, even my twin brother's.

When the parents themselves doubt their own physical attractiveness, inevitably they will unwittingly transfer that insecurity onto their children. For example, some parents compensate for their own insecurities by living their lives through the physical beauty or handsomeness of a daughter or son. Others show their insecurity by their inability to hold their children or verbally affirm their children in the unique beauty and the rightness of their bodies. I recall the case of a young professional married woman who came to me following the birth of her second child. She told me how she would get into a rage when people came up to the baby's cot saying, 'my God, she's beautiful and she looks just like your husband'. I asked her how she would feel if the people had said the child looked like her. 'I'd feel great', she replied. What was sad was that she had had the same experience with the first child and, as a result, had subconsciously distanced herself emotionally from both children. Even more sadly she was planning to have a third baby in the hope that at least she would have one child who looked like her. This woman's image of her own body was very poor and she was looking for acceptance of her physical self through her children. When that acceptance was not forthcoming, it confirmed her worst fears about her own physical self.

If a parent asks me, 'who does the baby look like?', I always say that the child looks remarkably like himself. It is a comment that does not go down very well but I follow up by saying that it is best that the child discovers his own uniqueness and does not feel that he is like somebody else.

It makes a considerable difference to school-going children if they enter the classroom with a strong sense of their unique physical selves and the rightness of their bodies. Such children have a much happier and easier experience of school than do children who are preoccupied with inner turmoil concerning their physical selves. The more the child has been convinced of the 'wrongness' of his body, the more difficult it will be to concentrate on the cognitive activity of school learning.

The emotional aspect of self

Children need to know that they are loved for themselves. This issue has been discussed in detail in earlier sections on the nature of unconditional and conditional love (pp. 50–57) and how family members communicate with each other (pp. 58–71). You will recall that there is only one kind of healthy loving and that is empathic and unconditional love. In this regard the message that parents and other adults need to communicate in their relationships with children is:

You unconditionally belong.

A child needs to feel that he is a special member of the family and that he has a special place in the home. Later on, the child will need to feel that he is a special member of the school class and that he has a special place in the school.

Because of conditionality on the part of their parents, many children do not feel they unconditionally belong to the family. Likewise, some children do not feel they have their own special place in the home because their parents are either perfectionist or neglectful and so do not help their children to create their own personal space within the home setting. The sense of belonging has two essential components:

Your presence matters and your absence matters.

Children need to feel that when they are in the home their presence matters and that when they are absent from the home they are missed. Children are quick to notice if they are being seen as a nuisance and even quicker to spot if adults breathe a sigh of relief when they are departing the scene. Such behaviours will result in children not feeling wanted and they may more frequently absent themselves from the home setting. One woman in her mid-thirties told me that when she was a young child she used to get up early in the morning, wash and dress herself, eat her breakfast and go away out for the day. As she related these experiences, she began to weep uncontrollably. What upset her most was that nobody ever followed to see whether she was hungry or in danger or lost. It was clear to her that her absence from the home did not matter a lot. She eventually went and talked out her feelings of rejection with her mother. Sadly, her mother retorted: 'well if I didn't love you then, I'm hardly going to start now'. Fortunately, my client had learned to love and accept herself at that stage and was able to stay separate from her mother's behaviour and not see it as 'rejection' but as a clear statement of the extremely poor self-esteem of her mother. Nonetheless, it was a deeply saddening experience.

Children need to be shown in a myriad of ways that they are loved for themselves. They need to be:

- Held
- Listened to
- Nurtured
- Talked to in positive ways
- Frequently shown unconditional love
- Played with
- Given treats

- Involved in parents' lives and have their parents involved in their lives
- Encouraged
- Affirmed
- Patiently and calmly responded to when showing difficult behaviour
- Shown empathy

Children who feel unconditionally loved and who feel that their presence in or absence from the home greatly matters are the children who come to school with high self-esteem and an openness to learning. Children who seriously doubt their lovability experience untold hidden emotional pain and will try all sorts of ways to resolve it. Their behaviours very often prevent them from being able to settle down to, what is for them, the less important task of educational development within the school. Unfortunately, teachers often unwittingly react punishingly to these children, thereby further deepening their emotional doubts about themselves.

The intellectual aspect of self

Children have limitless capacity to understand the world. However, in order to get in touch with that capacity, they need to first discover that they live in a safe and orderly world, where their essential needs are certain to be met. In their early relationships with children, parents and other significant adults need to communicate to them that:

You can make sense and order out of the world.

The key issue here is that children require to feel secure about getting their needs met. A baby has a few basic needs: to be held, to be fed, to have pain relieved and to be toileted. Babies are very active in their efforts to get their basic needs met: they wriggle, roll about, bang their heads, engage in different kinds of crying and so on. If their needs are met most of the time, babies begin to get a sense of being in a world that takes care of and is responsive to their needs. However, if needs are met only now and again, or even rarely, then nothing will later convince the child that he is living in a sensible and orderly world. As children get older, a whole array of physical, emotional, social, sexual, behavioural, creative and spiritual needs begins to emerge, and the extent and frequency of the response to these needs will determine the child's level of security. When children get older, it can be explained to them that, whilst they have every right to express any of their needs, it may not always be possible or feasible to meet them. Some needs cannot reasonably be met, if there are limited resources within the family. Children also need to discover that other people in the family have needs too, and that love, time, space, material resources, and so on are there for all members of the family.

When children come to school without being properly fed, washed, clothed or nurtured, they cannot attend to classwork. Many children in school are worried about needs that continue to go unmet and are struggling with not feeling wanted and feeling insecure in this world.

The behavioural aspect of self

Children will do anything to impress their parents and other significant adults. The main vehicle they use to impress is their behaviour. With regard to behaviour, the message that needs to be communicated to children is the double-barrelled one that:

You are capable in what you do and you please me.

It is not sufficient for parents, teachers and others to simply recognise the behavioural efforts of children, they also need to show that they are impressed by the child's person. When you recognise the effort, you increase the child's competence and by showing you are impressed by his person, you increase the child's confidence. There are many adults who possess genius and creative skills but who totally lack confidence in their abilities and who tend to 'hide their light under a bushel' or 'bury' their talents. The reason is that whilst parents may have acknowledged their attainments as children, they did not show they were impressed by their unique persons. Children who regularly experience this limited response to their efforts will persist but will never feel that they can behaviourally impress others.

Even more blocking of children's behavioural side of self is the situation where adults put the emphasis on performance rather than on effort. If the parent is critical or judgmental, this serves either to dry up children's efforts or to drive them into per-fectionism in an attempt to gain praise and attention. Parents and teachers need to always bear in mind that every effort is an attainment. When you acknowledge the attainment and show you are pleased by the child's effort, the child will eagerly move on to the next effort needed to bring about the next attainment step. However, if you confuse effort with performance, children become fearful of failure and mistakes and resort to the protective strategies of avoidance or compensation.

The second principle that parents and other adults need to bear in mind in their response to children's behavioural efforts is success and failure are relative terms. This is a critical issue and it needs to be pointed out to children that everybody, including the parent, has both success and failure experiences. Children need to be helped to understand that these terms are not absolutes and that nobody is either completely successful or a total failure. Success and failure only describe a particular behaviour but never a person.

A third principle deriving from the relativity of success and failure is mistakes and failures are opportunities for learning. Most people dread failure and mistakes and are very punishing, either of themselves or of others, when they occur. These same adults will often label children as lazy and apathetic when they do not make responsible academic efforts, and yet they rarely take any risks themselves. I have worked with some parents and teachers who believe that children need to be criticised in order 'to harden them up'. Ironically, these teachers and parents themselves tend to be hypersensitive to criticism. There is nothing further from the truth than that criticism strengthens a person. In fact, the opposite is true: criticism seriously weakens children's belief in their capacity, and either closes the door to behavioural development or drives them into unhappy overambition, perfectionism, overwork and a terror of failure. Parents strengthen children by putting them in touch with their limitless capacity to learn, by encouraging them to maintain their efforts, by applauding each effort as an attainment and by gently guiding them to the next required effort. At all times, the parent is firm that children meet assigned academic and other responsibilities.

The social aspect of self

Once, following a football match, I wandered across the road to a pub. While sitting up at the bar a fellow sportsman, in his best Cork accent, began to talk to me: 'great match boy', he said and I replied 'yes' and talked on about aspects of the game. At one stage he said to me, 'you know, a very strange thing, I was watching them all come out of the match, thousands of them, and Jesus, they were all different'. He was totally right, every person is uniquely different. You can travel the whole world and you will not find another exactly like you. Children need to be affirmed in their uniqueness. They need to know that there is room in their relationship with you for them to be different in values, perception, feelings and physical attributes. They need to be helped to learn at their particular pace and to do things in their own special way. However, difference is not generally encouraged and celebrated in our culture; instead conformity and sameness are much more strongly reinforced. What a boost to a child's self-worth to frequently hear from parents and other adults:

You are one of a kind and special.

In experiencing separation and difference from you, children need to know that they do not jeopardise their relationship with you. Children are often criticised or compared with others in terms of their size, shape, hair colour, eye colour, ways of seeing and doing things. Such responses may foster conformity or rebelliousness but, in neither case, do the children develop a strong sense of their own uniqueness. Children need to be encouraged to be comfortable with and accepting of their specialness. Comparisons with others greatly undermine children's self-worth and it is important to keep in mind that an act of comparison is an act of rejection.

A comment such as 'why aren't you neat and studious like your brother?' is practically guaranteed to drive a child into exactly the opposite behaviour. Every child has a deeply driven need to be different. The last thing the child wants is to be like someone else. If children go down the road of trying to be like somebody else (and some children are forced to be like their parents or other siblings), they will have no sense of individuality and will be highly dependent on others for acceptance. Some children sadly drop out under such pressure by seeking oblivion and rarely asserting their own unique identity.

The children who come to school with confidence in their uniqueness and specialness will find it much easier to adapt and to progress than children who are shy and introverted or who are loud and extroverted. The latter tend to pile up social problems for themselves which block concentration or else lead to anxiety and overemphasis on school work.

The creative aspect of self

Parents need to help children find and pursue their own unique life pattern. The message that children need to receive to realise their creative side is:

You have a right to your own unique growing.

Parents or teachers who dominate and control prevent the development of the child's unique growing and, consequently, seriously limit the child's expression of her uniqueness. There are many parents who force their own ambitions on children. I have worked with many adolescents and adults who were pursuing study and career paths that they actually had no leaning towards, but felt compelled to follow as their parents would be either tremendously disappointed or terribly angry and rejecting if they chose otherwise. Many parents want their children to have the opportunities and accomplishments they did not have; they think they are doing it all for the children, but, if the truth be told, they are doing it for themselves. They forget to ask the children what *they* want.

Children could be helped enormously to grow in self-esteem if parents encouraged them to pursue what 'fits' for them rather than trying to live other people's lives and responding to others' dependency needs. Children who pursue their own unique life-path retain high motivation for learning, but the converse is also true. Even if children go along with parents who dominate and control how they live their lives, there will be hidden resentment and always there will be a lack of self-fulfilment. When you have been living another person's life how can you ever feel self-actualised?

Parents need to be observant of and attentive to the unique aspects of their children's personalities: their interests and hobbies, their special ways of doing and seeing things, their ways of caring for and helping others, their ways of solving problems, the people they like to be with, the books, television programmes, music, academic subjects in which they show greatest interest and so on. Affirm them in their uniqueness and you set them up for a fulfilling life. Criticise, block, compare or threaten and you are likely to lose your relationship with your child and doom him to a life of conformity to the wishes and demands of others, with a deaf ear to his own unique development.

MORE WAYS OF MIRRORING A CHILD'S SELF-WORTH

There are many other actions on the part of parents that can mirror the self-worth of children:

- being genuine and sincere
- allowing personal time and space with each child
- sharing their lives with children
- asking children for help and advice
- asking rather than commanding that needs be met
- positive non-verbal and verbal behaviour.

Being genuine means being a 'real' person and not, for example, hiding behind 'parental authority' or your sheer physical size compared to children. It means being honest, open and spontaneous and staying separate in your communication with your children. It is essential to stay separate and to realise that your child's behaviour is always saying something about him and not about you as a parent. Many parents feel hurt, angry and rejected by their children's behaviours; this comes from failure to stay separate. When you fail to remain separate, you are likely to become defensive, and conflict between you and your child inevitably ensues. This conflict undermines the child's self-worth. Being genuine demands that parents are honest in their assessment of themselves and do not project their insecurities onto their children.

Allowing personal time and space with each child does much for the child to realise his self-worth. The issue here is that the closer the parental relationship with the child, the more it convinces the child of his worthiness. The child with middle to low self-esteem needs far more personal contact than the child with middle to high self-esteem. This personal time is not meant to be of an invasive nature, but one where genuine interest, concern and affection are shown towards the child.

Children love to hear stories of their parents' own life histories. They also like parents to bring them to their workplaces or places they socially frequent, and to involve them in their sports and leisure activities. All of this sharing lets children know that they matter in your life, and it affirms their image of themselves.

Another way to help children manifest a stronger sense of their capability is to ask them for their help and their opinions on issues. Giving children responsibility communicates belief in their resource-fulness and requesting their opinion elevates both their sense of belonging and their sense of capability. It is important that help and advice are asked for and not commanded. When parents make requests, they show respect for the child's right to freedom of response and they show that children have equal status in the relationship. When parents command, dominate and control they increase children's protectors and lower children's self-esteem.

Finally, parents need to guard against non-verbal and verbal messages that are blocking a child's self-worth. Children are very sensitive to the non-verbal language of parents and others. These non-verbal clues may communicate messages to children along the dimensions of:

- like–dislike
- interested–not interested
- superior–inferior.

Examples of non-verbal language are body posture, eye contact or lack of it, body orientation, tone of voice, pauses in speech, physical distance from the other, speed of speech, mannerisms, facial expression and gestures. Verbal messages are more obvious and it can be seen more clearly how they can enhance or reduce self-esteem. It is essential that verbal messages are of a positive nature such as praising, encouraging, welcoming, affirming, valuing, calming and caring. Be sure that the verbal message you give is in keeping with your non-verbal communication. If there is a difference or contradiction between the two levels of communication, the child will nearly always pick up on the non-verbal message. The body does not lie, but words can!

KEY INSIGHTS

☐ The level of self-esteem of the child determines not only educational progress but also emotional, social, intellectual, sexual, career and spiritual growth.

☐ The mirroring of children's self-worth is primarily in the hands of parents.

☐ The messages children more typically receive undermine, weaken, distort or even destroy any good sense of self.

- With regard to the mirroring of the self-worth of children there can be no such thing as benign neglect.
- The child's body is always right.
- Aggression breeds aggression.
- Children frequently blame themselves when they are neglected by parents or other significant adults in their lives.
- When parents doubt the rightness of their own bodies, they unwittingly transfer insecurity onto their children.
- Every child deserves to unconditionally belong to the family, home, classroom and school.
- Both the child's presence and absence always needs to matter in the family.
- The child who does not feel loved at home will present with difficulties in learning or overly diligent application in the school situation.
- Children have limitless capacity to make sense and order out of their world but they need their parents' help to realise this.
- The feeling of security, that the world is a safe and orderly place, is determined by how well the child's needs are met.
- Recognition of effort increases a child's competence and showing that the parent is impressed by the child's person increases the child's confidence.
- Every effort is an attainment.
- Success and failure are relative terms.
- Mistakes and failures are opportunities for learning.
- An act of comparison is an act of rejection.
- Every child has a deeply driven need to express his own unique person.
- Every child is one of a kind and special.
- Every child has a right to his own unique growing.
- Non-verbal communication is always stronger than verbal communication.

KEY ACTIONS

- Pay attention to your children's self-worth and you will greatly aid their educational development.
- Respond positively to your children's bodily symptoms as these are a revelation of unmet needs or hidden conflicts.
- Allow children to do what they can do for themselves.
- Respect, accept and value your own body and your children will be likely to do the same.
- Avoid criticism, comparisons and 'smart' remarks with regard to your children's bodies; these hurt far more than you may realise.
- Regularly – physically and verbally – show your children unconditional love.
- Let your children know that both their presence and absence matter to you.
- Let each child know that he is a special member of the family and has his own special place in the home.
- Do your best to meet as many as you can of the reasonable needs of your children.
- Regularly recognise and praise your children's efforts to grow in this world.
- Let your children know that every effort of theirs is an attainment.
- Never ridicule or scold children for mistakes and failures.
- Help your children to learn and grow from mistakes and failures.
- Do not compare one child with another.
- Let your children regularly know that they are unique – a once-off happening, never to be repeated in this universe.
- Help your children to discover their own unique ways of being in this world, their unique ambitions, talents, aspirations, perceptions and so on.

- ☐ Be genuine and sincere in your interactions with your children.
- ☐ Frequently affirm your child's person.
- ☐ Spend personal time with each child.
- ☐ Make requests, not commands.

CHAPTER 7

HELPING THE CHILD
WHO IS TROUBLED

TROUBLED BEHAVIOURS ARE ALWAYS RIGHT

Irish society has radically changed in the last two decades. The increase in marital breakdown and marital separation, the increase of lone-parent families, the rise of materialism, the decline of religion, the advent of a pluralist society, high unemployment and the increase in academic demands and pressures are all leading to an increase in the rate of troubled behaviour among children. Emotional conflict in children is not new – there have always been problematic marriages and families with consequent blocking effects on the self-worth of children. But the point is that pressures have increased. It is now estimated that anything up to 30 per cent of children are suffering inner conflicts that need professional intervention.

Traditionally, when children presented with difficult behaviours in the home, they were met with an authoritarian response. This does not and never did work, and neither is it desirable. Domination of a child may produce fear and silence but it brings about no reduction in the inner conflict of the child; indeed it serves only to increase that conflict. Furthermore, dominating and controlling behaviours are protective means of communication and always mean that the mature development of both children and parents is blocked. Many parents have not learned constructive and caring approaches to children's problematic behaviours whether within or outside the home. A full understanding of the nature of troubled behaviours among children provides a solid basis for the development of appropriate responses.

The first insight needed is that children's problematic behaviours are always right. Sounds like a paradox, does it not? How could behaviours such as bedwetting, fidgeting, hyperactivity, nail biting, argumentativeness, temper tantrums and so on be right? The answer is that these difficult behaviours are signs of underlying conflict within children. The problematic actions are not the problem but revelations or manifestations of it. Unfortunately, because these behavioural manifestations, particularly when they are undercontrol behaviours, disrupt the household they become a problem to parents and other members of the family. The typical reaction is to punish them. However, in spite of the punishment, the behaviours will tend to persist because the hidden conflict has not been identified but has actually been increased. The following examples illustrate the process.

A mother brought me her fourteen-year-old daughter who was regularly stealing from her classmates, from family members and from relatives. Strangely, she rarely got away with the stealing. In spite of being threatened, shouted at, criticised, labelled, deprived of privileges and slapped, the stealing had by now persisted for several years. When I spoke to the girl on her own, one of the things she said convinced me that the answer to her problem lay in her past and was somehow being continually re-enacted in the present. What she said was: 'for years I just cannot help myself from getting into trouble, it is as if there is something inside me driving me to be troublesome'. How accurate she was unknowingly.

When she was seven years of age a younger sister, aged three years, had suddenly died. Both parents had adored this child and her death seemed to cause an emotional death within each of them. The remaining daughter, my client, had deeply loved her little sister and was highly traumatised by her death. She also had some unresolved guilt feelings about having hit her sister a week before her death. She had never been allowed to talk out her grief or guilt or the other feelings she had about her sister. Neither had she been allowed to go to her sister's funeral. She had been sent off to an aunt and returned home a week later. Her sister's name was never brought up again within the family. Both of her parents became emotionally closed off from her. It seemed to me that not only had this child had her sister stolen from her but also the love of her parents. It was as if she had lost three people in one fell swoop. Other things also were stolen from her: her right to grieve, to talk about her sister and to let go of her guilt feelings. The stealing started within six months of the death of her sister and had persisted for seven years.

The parents were very cooperative, coming in for therapy for themselves and gradually becoming a warm, loving and closely-knit family again. They also began to talk about the dead child and gave freedom to their daughter to do the same. The stealing stopped; it had fulfilled its purpose. The hidden conflict within this child was now revealed and, most importantly, was being given an appropriate response.

You have seen other examples throughout this book of how children's problematic behaviours are always right. You will recall the case where the child's bedwetting was a revelation of his not feeling loved and wanted by his father; the case where the child holding his faeces was a manifestation of not being given enough freedom to explore his world; and the case where the child's soiling was a revelation of nobody caring for him. Another example is the child who is overly diligent and perfectionist, which are manifestations of the hidden conflicts of fear of failure, dependence on performance and a deep fear of rejection.

Problematic behaviours then are always right because they reveal the inner conflicts and unmet needs of children. It is important to realise that the child is not deliberately engaging in these difficult behaviours but knows of no other way to get her needs met. More than likely, adaptive ways did not work in the home for the child and, in desperation, the maladaptive ways developed as a last resort. Problematic behaviours are signs and it is most important that they are not displayed in vain. Nevertheless, the same behaviours are also socially 'unacceptable' because they can make life very difficult for parents and other family members. For example, a three-year-old child who 'has it in' for her baby brother is a threat to the well-being of the infant and a source of great distress to the parents. It is important to bear in mind that the hidden conflict is different for or unique to each child so that there is no one way of responding to children's troubled behaviours.

If a child's problematic behaviour is right, why then is it generally called maladaptive? Take the case of a child who whines continually throughout the day. The whining is maladaptive because, even though the child may get some attention by employing such behaviour, it never resolves the child's underlying conflict and indeed – and this is the crunch point – it often increases the hidden insecurities. When a child constantly whines, very often the parent gets irritated and will, for example, shout at the child, 'will you stop that whining, you're driving me insane?' Such a response plunges the child back into her frightening conviction that she is not loved and so the insecurity increases. Similarly, children who are aggressive and disruptive are very often revealing hurt and anger because many of their needs to be loved, cared for, affirmed, nurtured, protected, given freedom and challenge are not being met by parents. Unfortunately, the aggressive and disruptive means used to act out these unmet needs, result in further punishment by parents and so the hidden conflicts remain.

RECOGNITION OF SIGNS OF CHILDREN'S DISTRESS

It is important that parents pick up on the early signs of the development of self-esteem protectors in children and immediately begin to take corrective action. It is not difficult for parents to identify the child who is troubled. There are multiple manifestations of self-esteem protectors among children. If such emotional, social, and behavioural signs are regularly shown, then appropriate and constructive responses are needed, whether this be in the home, school or neighbourhood, or some combination of these three.

Signs of children's hidden conflict may be categorised under three main headings:

- physical signs
- undercontrol signs
- overcontrol signs.

It is important to note that physical signs may also be manifested by children displaying undercontrol or overcontrol signs of inner conflict. In Chapter 6 you saw that the child's body is always right and attention to bodily signs is a very accurate means of getting to the child's emotional insecurity.

Signs of undercontrol include those behaviours that may be very troublesome and annoying to others but are, nonetheless, clear signs of emotional distress. Children displaying these signs are acting out their inner turmoil in a subconscious attempt to get their unmet needs recognised and met. Typical undercontrol signs are rebellious behaviours, verbal aggressiveness, destructiveness of property, hyperactivity and bullying. Psychologically, these distressing behaviours are saying something right about the child but, socially, the behaviours can make it extremely difficult for parents. The danger is that parents can respond protectively to these manifestations, thereby adding fuel to the fire, with the resultant escalation of the child's undercontrol behaviours. The 'out-of-control' punishing response by parents serves only to convince the child of her inadequacy and unlovability, and plunges her into further depths of insecurity. Because children's undercontrol behaviours can be so upsetting to the other family members, some action is of course needed to try to reduce or eliminate them. But this action needs to be carried out in conjunction with attempts to discover what is emotionally troubling the child. It is interesting, and also understandable, that children who show undercontrol behaviours are those who are most frequently referred for professional help. It is also of note that boys are more likely than girls to act out their inner turmoil through undercontrol behaviours.

Girls are more likely than boys to exhibit overcontrol manifestations of emotional conflict. Examples include shyness, perfectionism, withdrawal from social situations and extreme attempts to please others; they do not in any serious way disrupt the lives of others. Quiet, shy children do not interfere with parents in carrying out their domestic and other responsibilities. Frequently such children are not seen as troubled and consequently do not get the help they require. Unfortunately, these children are often more at risk emotionally than those children who 'act out' their feelings of rejection and inadequacy. It is as if those who shout the loudest are most likely to be heard. It is important therefore that parents and other adults are vigilant for overcontrol signs of emotional conflict, and try to disover and lovingly respond to the child's underlying unmet needs.

The hope is that children, whether they display undercontrol or overcontrol behaviours, will have their emotional conflicts detected and appropriately responded to, and that more adaptive ways of expressing their fears, worries and insecurities will be taught to them. There is no doubt that parents and teachers are becoming more aware and more concerned about the mirroring of children's self-worth, and want to know more about how to create loving relationships within the home and school.

Typical signs of distress among children are outlined below. A child who is regularly showing two or more of these behaviours is manifesting clear signs of hidden emotional conflict.

TYPICAL SIGNS OF CHILDREN'S INNER CONFLICT

Physical signs

- ☐ Nail biting
- ☐ Bedwetting
- ☐ Soiling
- ☐ Facial grimaces
- ☐ Involuntary muscle spasms
- ☐ Restlessness
- ☐ Stammering
- ☐ Sudden flushing or paling
- ☐ Poor physical coordination
- ☐ Affectations or posturings
- ☐ Frequent complaints of headaches or abdominal pain
- ☐ Obesity
- ☐ Loss of weight
- ☐ Poor appetite

- [ ] Jumping at sudden noises
- [ ] Low energy
- [ ] Skin problems
- [ ] Insomnia

Undercontrol signs

Personal signs: child
- [ ] Behaviour too young for age
- [ ] Hyperactivity
- [ ] Irresponsible behaviour
- [ ] Impulsive behaviour
- [ ] Mischievousness
- [ ] Clinging behaviour
- [ ] Carelessness about homework
- [ ] Overexcitability
- [ ] Uncontrolled laughing or giggling
- [ ] Highly distractible
- [ ] Extravagant emotional expression
- [ ] Frequent nightmares
- [ ] Speaking too fast
- [ ] Destructiveness of own or other people's property
- [ ] Defacing of books
- [ ] Abusive, vulgar or obscene language
- [ ] Writing obscenities on walls
- [ ] Frequent minor delinquencies
- [ ] Lying
- [ ] Cheating
- [ ] Thieving

☐ Hatred of school work

☐ Not listening

☐ Not benefiting from experience

☐ Blaming of others for mistakes and failures

☐ Highly critical of others

☐ Show-off

☐ Playing truant from school

Interpersonal signs: parents

☐ Frequent requests for help

☐ Attention-seeking

☐ Efforts to curry favour with parents

☐ Frequently argumentative

☐ Disruptive of parents' activities

☐ Makes many requests for special attentions and favours

☐ Gives irrelevant answers to questions

☐ Acts tough

☐ Exaggerated courtesy

☐ Constant bragging

☐ Hostile reactions to criticism

☐ Frequent justification of self

☐ Misinterpretation of what parents say

☐ False accusations of parents or others

☐ Frequent complaints of unfair treatment

☐ Complaints that parents 'have it in' for her

☐ Insolence

☐ Temper tantrums or aggressive outbursts when corrected or requested to do something

- Resentment of parents
- Unwillingness to share domestic responsibilities
- Hostile response to behavioural management

Interpersonal signs: siblings and other children

- Bullying
- Teasing
- Pushiness
- Trying to be funny
- Acting tough
- Dominating and controlling younger siblings or other smaller children
- Showing off
- Abusive or obscene language
- Frequent verbal and physical 'fights' with siblings or peers
- Regular complaints that other children do not like her
- Frequent relaying of 'dirty' stories
- Overinterest in sexual matters

Overcontrol signs

Personal signs: child

- Extreme shyness
- Poor or no self-confidence
- Strong tendency to remain alone
- Homesickness
- School 'phobia'
- High insecurity and anxiety
- Timidity

☐ Fearfulness of new challenges

☐ Mutism

☐ Avoidance of games

☐ Tendency not to mix with other children

☐ Overstudious

☐ Frequent day-dreaming

☐ Worrying unduly

☐ Frequently looking sad

☐ Poor motivation to learn

☐ Appears 'lost in another world'

☐ Obsessional and/or compulsive behaviours

☐ Overly exact

☐ Meticulous

☐ Undue anxiety over school examinations

☐ Undue distress over failures and mistakes

☐ Preoccupation with scholastic results

☐ Being the 'perfect' child or student

☐ Overabsorption in hobby or interest

Interpersonal signs: parents

☐ Feelings easily hurt

☐ Hypersensitive to criticism

☐ Little or no eye contact

☐ Few or no requests for help

☐ Extreme nervousness when answering questions

☐ Poor response to affirmation and praise

☐ Wanting to please at all times

☐ Irrelevant answers to questions

- ☐ Failure to respond when spoken to
- ☐ Frequent breaking off of speech in the middle of a sentence
- ☐ Mental blocks when either answering questions or doing an examination

Interpersonal signs: siblings and other children
- ☐ Few or no friends
- ☐ Overt rejection by peers
- ☐ Fading into background when siblings are present
- ☐ Avoidance of team games
- ☐ Frequent target of fun
- ☐ Absence from community or school events

Each child's problem is peculiar to her home surroundings and has to be understood and responded to within that special context. Nevertheless, we know that all children who manifest troubled behaviours, such as those listed above, inevitably have self-esteem screens which are directly and closely related to their inner conflicts.

CAUSES OF CHILDHOOD PROBLEMS

Some of the possible causes of childhood conflict are outlined below. It is important, however, to keep in mind that the source of each child's problem is unique to her life story. In the next section you will see that getting to the unique causes of an individual child's protective behaviours is crucial to resolving her inner conflicts.

The sources of childhood problems may be usefully categorised under the following headings:

- – inside the family
- – within the child

- inside the school
- outside home and school.

Causes inside the family

Emotional and behavioural problems among children arise primarily from what happens inside the family:

- how the parents relate to each other
- how the parents relate to the children
- loss of parents through death, separation or divorce
- parents' own self-esteem problems
- protective behaviours of parents
- lack of continuous relationship with mother or mother substitute in the first three years of life
- modelling by parents of socially unacceptable behaviours
- poor parenting skills
- subcultural home background whose values, morals, and standards differ from those of the larger culture into which children need to fit as they grow up.

Children depend on both parents for love and security and become very troubled when parents relate to each other in hostile ways, when there is violence or silences that go on for weeks on end, or when there are frequent arguments. Marital conflict is a major source of stress in children's lives and, whether the partners choose to stay with each other or not, what is essential for the welfare of the children is that conflict ceases.

The major cause of children's problems is how their parents relate to them. When parents are dominating, controlling, hypercritical or grossly neglectful, children become tremendously insecure and will manifest their feelings of rejection through undercontrol or overcontrol protective behaviours.

The loss of a parent or parents, particularly in the first five years of life, may be a major pressure for children. The person who gives care, and the nature of that care, following a parent's death will greatly determine whether the loss of the parent remains a stressful influence on their development and growth.

You have seen that when parents themselves have self-esteem protectors they, albeit unknowingly, project their insecurities not only onto their partners but also onto their children. Low self-esteem of parents is the source of both conditional loving of children and their total neglect. It has already been shown how conditional loving affects children in terms of engendering fears and depression (see pp. 50–57).

Some parents exhibit problematic behaviours that can have devastating effects on the self-esteem of children. Typical examples are drunkenness, violence, sexual abuse, frequent irritability, depression, timidity, passivity, chronic insecurity, anorexia and psychosomatic illnesses.

There is considerable evidence that when children do not experience a continuous relationship with one adult carer for the first three years of life, they become chronically insecure and have difficulty in forming close emotional relationships with others. Examples of such children may be found in orphanages where children have no close relationship with any one adult. There are many reasons why such children become either totally withdrawn or extremely hostile: they have experienced loss of love, have many unmet needs, and feel they are members of a world that is not safe or orderly. Moreover, they have learned that the way to avoid any further hurt, humiliation and rejection is not to take any risks of reaching out for love and acceptance. These children are not irredeemable but great patience and enduring love are needed to break through the protective shell they have created for themselves.

Children imitate their parents' behaviours and when parents engage regularly in socially unacceptable behaviours, the likelihood of children repeating these patterns is very high. Examples of such behaviour are verbal aggression, violence, passivity, protective communication patterns, irresponsibility, loudness, vulgarity, overeating and gambling.

Let me repeat that parenting is the hardest job of all. Yet it is the only profession for which no training is provided. The responsibilities of parents are enormous and the results of their lack of knowledge of parenting skills can be devastating to the development of both themselves and their children. Parenting is not an instinctive skill. Human behaviour is far too complex psychologically and socially for parents to rely only on biological instincts and drives. Parenting courses are now widely available and often well attended but sadly those parents who most need help rarely attend. This is understandable; the threat to their self-worth in attending such courses would be very great. People with low self-esteem will subconsciously do anything to keep their feelings of inferiority hidden, and avoidance is one of the greatest protectors of all. A lot of safety is needed for such parents to attend parenting and personal development courses.

Another cause of children's problems arising from within the family is being a member of a subculture. The difficulties arise when such children are expected to become part of the larger culture. Inevitably, children from the subculture will notice the difference between them and their peers from the larger cultural group. This difference becomes a source of anxiety and insecurity, and some of them become 'drop-outs' early on, withdrawing their allegiance from the larger culture. However, when their own culture is respected and valued and their differences are not criticised, these children will begin to absorb knowledge and feel free to make their own life choices later on.

Causes within the child

Childhood problems may also arise from causes within children themselves:

- poor self-esteem
- physical or mental disability
- developmental delays
- poor knowledge levels.

The most typical cause of problems arising within children is poor feelings about themselves. When children perceive themselves as unlovable or inadequate they will act in ways that accord with these low opinions of themselves. Unless these images change, the children are doomed to a very difficult life. The most effective way to change the images children have of themselves is to change the nature of the interactions between them and the significant adults in their lives. Once these interactions are of an unconditionally loving nature and are affirming and encouraging, the opinion the children hold of themselves will slowly but surely begin to change.

Some children are, unfortunately, mentally or physically disadvantaged. At least one-third of these children also experience psychological and social difficulties. Helping them to accept and cope with their disadvantage is a necessary part of the parenting and teaching of these children. When they are truly loved for themselves it is less likely that they will develop psychological and social difficulties.

Some children may experience developmental delays and, when they go to school, may have poorer physical coordination and poorer reading and language abilities, and overall may be markedly different in behaviour from their peers. The children themselves may become self-conscious of these differences, but the situation is made even worse if parents or teachers are critical of them or push them, as then their self-esteem is affected and consequently emotional, social and more learning difficulties will arise.

Children may have low knowledge levels if they come from homes where reading, stimulation, education, language development and the teaching of skills for independent living are not strongly present or valued. Such children will be at a disadvantage when they go into school and other social situations and may, as a consequence, suffer ridicule or criticism. This leads to self-consciousness and feelings of inferiority, and avoidance or aggressive strategies may emerge to protect from further hurt and rejection.

Causes inside the school

Most of us have had teachers whom we fondly remember but it is also true that many of us have had neglectful experiences in school. There are teachers who, because of their own self-esteem protectors, have had devastating effects on the self-esteem of their students. Causes of conflict arising within the school include:

- fear of the teacher
- fear of examinations
- fear of standing up and speaking in class
- fear of other students.

Teachers who are feared by children display a range of behaviours that seriously block children's self-worth: criticism, dominance, sarcasm, cynicism, ridicule, scolding, impatience, intolerance, authoritarianism, irritability and verbal (and sometimes physical) aggressiveness. All of these behaviours precipitate either under-control behaviours or withdrawal and silent resentment on the part of the victimised students and they are always emotionally disruptive: the students who are passive and quiet get hurt, those who are verbally quick 'talk back' and those who are hostile make scenes. Each of these reactions is a clear sign to the teacher and to the children's parents that the relationship between the teacher and the students needs to be changed. If the relationship does not change, everybody in this classroom loses out.

Fear of examinations is an all too common problem within the school setting. Its effects are well known: anxiety, concentration problems, memory difficulties, insomnia, headaches, muscle tension, 'mental blocks', depression, suicidal feelings and so on. This fear comes from excessive pressure on children for examination marks by parents or teachers or both.

Some children, particularly in early adolescence, have a fear of standing up and speaking in class. This may stem from, for example, sensitivity over height or voice change. Teachers need to be sensitive to this difficulty and try to make classwork as informal as possible. In younger children such fear may indicate poor self-esteem and a dread of failure and of making a fool of themselves.

Bullying has become another all too common behaviour within the school setting. Bullying produces fear in the victims, it may lead to refusal to go to school and, certainly, leads to insecurity and un-happiness with regard to attending school. The children who bully are in need of psychological help but their manner of expressing their self-esteem difficulties cannot be allowed to continue as it leads to other students also displaying problematic behaviours.

Causes outside home and school

Inner conflict can also arise from problems associated with persons or situations outside the home or the school. Examples include:

- hostile neighbours
- victimisation by other children
- emotional, physical or sexual violation by a relative, child-minder or person living in the community
- peer group pressure.

There are children who are terrified by hostile neighbours and nervous of going outdoors; as a result, they can miss out on social, emotional and physical developments that come about through playing and interacting with other children. Similarly, when children are fearful of being victimised by other children in the neigh-bourhood they too may miss out on peer interactions. In both cases, parents need to take strong action to ensure safety for their children. Sometimes children may be violated physically, emotionally or sexually by an adult well known to the family. Such hidden neglect will have marked effects on children's emotional well-being. It is essential for parents to create a climate of safety, where the children have permission to talk out any difficulty they may be having with any adult, so that this situation is less likely to occur. When children fail to find security in the home they will frequently attempt to find it within their peer group, and will conform and be loyal to the activities of this group whether these be of a positive or delinquent nature. Unless matters change at home they are unlikely to let go of this source of security and acceptance.

RESPONDING TO SIGNS OF DISTRESS IN CHILDREN

The process underlying an understanding of children's problematic or protective behaviours can be illustrated as follows:

Level 1: Problematic behaviours

Level 2: Signs/revelations

Level 3: Unique underlying conflict

Demanding unique responses from parents/teachers/
significant others

Parents need to respond to children's problematic behaviours at each of the levels: focusing on level 1, without exploring the signals at level 2 and identifying and responding to level 3, is unlikely to be successful.

Parental response to children's protective behaviours (level 1)

Typically, breakdown in responding to children's distress occurs at level 1 – the level where, for example, temper tantrums, fidgeting, involuntary muscular spasms, bedwetting and stealing are being manifested – so that levels 2 and 3 are rarely reached. It is important when a child manifests a problematic behaviour that the parents do not get into conflict with her. When the parents respond with an 'out-of-control' behaviour, they are showing signs of their own self-esteem difficulties by personalising the child's difficult behaviours. The secret is to stay separate from the child's problematic behaviour and, when the child is calm, try in a relaxed and loving way to discover what the behaviours are saying about the child. The hidden issues will nearly always relate to a self-esteem problem, but the causes of this problem need to be discovered (for example, favouritism, never feeling good enough, feeling compared with and inferior to a sibling, corporal punishment, sexual violation).

Reasoning with a child, or even approaching the child with warmth and affection, will not work if she is out of control because, as said before, emotions are always stronger than reason. The best action in such circumstances is no action. Stay calm, stay separate; only when the child has regained control do you move to level 2 and attempt to explore the self-esteem protectors and hidden conflicts. No matter how difficult the troublesome behaviours manifested at level 1, it is rarely of any help to punish these behaviours as all you are doing is suppressing or eliminating the very avenues which will lead you into the child's hidden insecurities. Consequently, things may go from bad to worse or the child may totally withdraw physically and emotionally from you.

PRINCIPLES OF EFFECTIVE PARENTAL RESPONSE TO CHILDREN'S PROTECTIVE BEHAVIOURS

- Do not get into conflict with the child.
- Stay calm and unflappable.
- Stay separate – do not personalise the child's behaviours as deliberate attempts to annoy or thwart you.
- If the child is manifesting undercontrol behaviours do nothing but maintain strong eye contact. Make no other verbal or non-verbal (for example, grimacing, sighing, clenching fists) response.
- Remove yourself from the child's presence when you feel you are beginning to lose control of your own responses.
- Explore what hidden conflicts are leading to the protective manifestations, when both the child and yourself are calm and in charge of yourselves.

If you feel you are going to lose control, remove yourself immediately from the child. Staying separate and not being trapped into conflict with children can be very difficult; sometimes you will fail and respond in blaming, condemning and even aggressive ways with children who are troubled. If you do so, always apologise to the child after you have calmed down and let her know what led you to out-of-control behaviour. In doing this, you are healing the break in the relationship, you are demonstrating to the child how to communicate directly and clearly, and you are giving the important message that it is okay to fail at times.

Parental response to exploring children's hidden insecurities (level 2)

Do not be put off by children's reticence to revealing and exploring what is distressing and disturbing them. Children feel threatened by such revelations as they dread further hurt and rejection. They are terrified of discovering that maybe you really do not like or love them, that they are just not good enough, or that they are 'too ugly' or 'too stupid' to be acceptable. Once you gently persist in an unconditionally loving way, eventually the hidden fears will emerge. Do not force your way into the hidden world of children as this is neglectful and will only lead them into greater depths of secrecy. If, in spite of your best efforts, your children are not yet ready to reveal to you what is distressing them, then let them know that you understand what you are requesting may be difficult for them and that, whether or not they tell you, you love them and you are always there to listen when they are ready to talk. Creating safety for children to reveal their doubts and fears is essential.

Whether or not you discover the inner conflicts of your child, it is wise to look to yourself and see whether you are, on a daily basis, interacting with your child in ways that mirror her self-worth. If you have been neglecting such responsibilities then you now have some idea of what might be the source of your child's difficulties. Check out also your own feelings about yourself and see whether you may be projecting your insecurities onto your child by, for example, being neglectful, critical, dominating, controlling or overly protective.

PRINCIPLES FOR EXPLORING THE HIDDEN CONFLICTS OF CHILDREN

☐ Gently explore with the child what is leading to the persistent problematic and distressing behaviours.

☐ Do not force your way into the child's hidden world (by commanding, directing, interrogating, threatening, becoming annoyed or irritated).

☐ Be patient and allow your child all the time and space she needs before revealing inner fears and insecurities.

☐ Create safety in the home and give permission for your child to be direct and open about unmet needs and conflicts.

☐ Reassure your child that she is always loved, and that you are there and ready to listen any time she needs to talk.

☐ Look to yourself in terms of how you generally interact with the child who is presenting with problems.

☐ Immediately and persistently engage in behaviours that mirror your child's self-worth.

☐ Check out your own level of self-esteem and ensure that you are not projecting your insecurities onto your child.

☐ Model adaptive ways for your child to get her needs met and talk out difficult issues.

A valuable way to help children to talk out their fears and insecurities is for you to model direct and open communication on such issues. For example, if you have a difficulty with some person, show your children how you own your own issues and how you reveal them in a way that does not blame or hurt the other person. Show your children how you clearly express your needs, fears and concerns but without pressurising the other person to respond to your unmet needs. It helps to tell children stories of your own childhood – times when you felt sad, rejected, lonely or lacking in ability – and how you wished you had talked these things out with your parents.

Parental response to uniqueness of children's conflicts (level 3)

Having dealt with levels 1 and 2 you need to take the further step of discovering the unique aspects of your child's problem so that you can directly target the areas for healing. Sometimes, it can happen that when you begin to engage in behaviours that mirror your child's self-worth, you accidentally hit on the hidden insecurity of the child and, when that happens, the signs of your child's distress will begin to disappear. However, that is a rare occurrence, and persistence is usually required to get to what is uniquely causing your child's distress. You have seen many examples of the uniqueness of children's problems throughout this book. Recall, for example, the three-year-old girl who was starving herself in order to please and look like her daddy and the child who lost his sight because he believed nobody would ever want to look at him.

A mother contacted me about her child who had gone off happily and enthusiastically to her first day in primary school. On returning at lunchtime the child was visibly upset, and when she was due to go back to school she disappeared; her mother eventually found her locked into a wardrobe. The child was convulsed with crying and refused to return to school. When her mother rang in a panic as to what she needed to do, I advised her not to force the child back to school. Something obviously had happened to undermine the child's earlier security, happiness and enthusiasm but the possibilities as to what exactly was the cause were endless – homesickness, bullying by other children, aggressiveness on the teacher's part, failure experience. I suggested that when the child had calmed down and the threat of returning to school had been removed, her mother request her to tell all the things that happened to her during the morning. It transpired that, no sooner had the children settled in class, than the teacher took out a big stick and, while waving it about, warned them that if they were bold the stick would be used on them. It was important that the child now got reassurance from her parents that nobody had a right to threaten her in any way. It was also vital that the relationship between the teacher and the child be corrected and that the teacher reassure the child that such an incident would not occur again. If, having approached the teacher on the matter, the threatening behaviour recurred, the child's welfare would be at risk and in such a case I would insist the child be removed from that teacher's class. Furthermore, if the school principal were not cooperative I would remove the child from the school. I would also report the teacher's illegal and irresponsible behaviour to the Department of Education and would not let the matter rest until appropriate action had been taken. Silence on such behaviours has gone on for far too long.

It is not possible to provide general guidelines for getting to the particular source of each child's problem as the parental responding required is unique to each child. Once you have discovered the unique causes of your child's distress then you can initiate appropriate healing actions to address the revealed conflict; all the time you persist in not getting trapped into conflict with the child, you work to affirm your child's and your own self-worth and you try to separate your own life from your child's.

If, in spite of your best efforts, a child's problematic behaviours continue, it may then be wise to seek professional help.

SEEKING PROFESSIONAL HELP

Deciding whether your child's problems require specialised help is not necessarily as easy as might be assumed. All the signs of children's distress illustrated in this chapter are, by and large, exaggerations or deficits of behaviour patterns common to all children. This section presents the main factors to consider before deciding whether the problems of your child need professional attention. It is wise to first consult with a specialist and having conferred on the problems only then, if requested, bring the child along for help. My own experience in working with children is that I only sometimes need to see the child. I work first with the parents to change their interactions – with each other or with the child or both. If such intervention does not change the child's level of distress, I will then ask to see the child.

There are a number of issues to be considered before making the decision to go to a specialist:

- age and stage of the child's development
- frequency of troubled behaviour
- intensity of troubled behaviour
- persistence of troubled behaviour
- child's home environment
- child's school and classroom environments
- whose help needs to be sought?

Age and stage of the child's development

In the case of many problematic behaviours, whether or not they are deemed to be in need of professional help depends on the child's age. Behaviours which are common and normal at some ages are problematic at others. For instance, temper tantrums are common in preschool children and many parents have experienced the so-called terrible twos. Bedwetting (nocturnal enuresis) occurs frequently in children up to the age of three or four years but it is clearly problematic in children of over five years and even more alarming in an adolescent. Younger children have many fears because they are still adjusting to aspects of their world, but school-going children who show fears of the dark, failure, animals, conflict or teachers and other children are clearly manifesting inner emotional or social problems.

Frequency of troubled behaviour

The more frequently a behavioural difficulty is occurring, the more likely it is that specialised help is required. The odd incident of disruptive behaviour or emotional and physical withdrawal may indicate only transient problems which clear up with the passage of time and experience.

Intensity of troubled behaviour

The more extreme the emotional intensity (for example, overwhelming anger, panic attacks) or the avoidance or aggressive reactions, the stronger the signs are that your child needs help. For instance, about one-third of children who show reluctance to attend school manifest severe distress and panic reactions when attempts are made to bring them to school. Excessive distress will manifest itself in the child's physiological state (for example, increased heart rate, paling, vomiting, abnormal pains, shaking), in verbally expressed feelings of fear and discomfort, and in strong attempts to avoid school.

Persistence of troubled behaviour

The more the difficult actions persist over time, the stronger the indications are that the child needs professional help. Many older children carry problems from their earlier years which, regrettably, were not picked up at the stage of onset. Secondary difficulties will have developed for these children as scholastically and socially they will often have fallen behind their peers, adding to their inner conflict and self-esteem protectors.

Child's home environment

I have already pointed out that it is my experience in working with some children that it is their parents who need help and not them. Very often, I do little to treat the children but put great emphasis on changing the relationships within the family which are determined by the parents' own levels of self-esteem. You have seen that many parents project their own insecurities, unmet needs, perfectionism, rigidity, anxieties, pessimism and helplessness onto children and, unless these problems are resolved, the children of these parents will continue to be at risk. The troubled behaviours of children can be a normal response to an abnormal home situation; the abnormality resides in the home environment rather than in the child. For example, a child's aggression may be a function of the blocking of her needs within a rigid, restrictive, dominating and controlling code of parental behaviours. Alternatively, a child's aggression may be the consequences of that child imitating parental behaviour. Furthermore, problematic behaviours of theft, delinquency and truancy in adolescents have been associated with parental attitudes of indifference. In these neglectful circumstances the adolescents, finding no love, acceptance and security in the home, will often seek recognition from their peer group and follow the behavioural patterns of that group. Within the peer group, activities such as theft, playing truant, destruction of property and aggression may be the norm – yet another example of the influence of the environment rather than pathology in relation to the problems of children.

Child's school and classroom environments

As you have already seen not all the troubled behaviours of children arise from their family circumstances. The school environment or a particular teacher's action may explain why a child is undergoing some emotional or behavioural problem. Children who come from a subculture may be under pressure to 'fit in' to the larger culture of the school. There are teachers (as in any other profession) who have their own deep, unresolved conflicts and these may manifest themselves in the classroom through modes of behaviour that are either aggressive, cynical, sarcastic and dominating or timid and fearful in nature. The effects of such behaviours on children's well-being may be great. Parents need to be vigilant of teachers who are troubled but who, nonetheless, need to be confronted on their behaviours (see pp. 203–7).

Whose help needs to be sought?

Most children who need specialist help are reacting with protective behaviour to some traumatic experience in the home, school, classroom or other setting in the present or past. As such, the preferred help is psychotherapy or family therapy. Drug treatment is not to be recommended. The last thirty years have seen the emergence of a variety of helping approaches: behaviour therapy, cognitive therapy, art therapy, drama therapy, gestalt psychotherapy, client-centred psychotherapy to mention but a few. These approaches either attempt to change the environment in which the child lives or deal directly with the child's emotional and behavioural difficulties. Family therapy involves treating the whole family and focusing on problems in the interactions between family members as the source of the child's problems.

These treatments are often effective and the high demand for them is indicative of that effectiveness. However, be sure to check out the professional person you decide to consult. Furthermore, if the problems continue despite genuine and sincere efforts by all parties, do not be afraid to suggest to the therapist that perhaps a different therapeutic approach might be more successful. Finally, it is my conviction that an understanding of the child's inner life, and that of her parents and of any other adult or peer group involved, must always precede the choice of therapeutic approach.

Generally speaking, your family doctor will be aware of who's who in the fields of psychoanalysis and psychotherapy in your geographical area and, if needed, will arrange a consultation for you.

KEY INSIGHTS

- Children's troubled behaviours are always right.
- Problematic behaviours of children are signs and it is most important that they are not displayed in vain.
- The hidden conflict of a child is unique to that child so that there is no one way to respond to children's problems.
- Problematic behaviours of children are always psychologically right but may be socially difficult, particularly undercontrol protective behaviours.
- Children showing undercontrol behaviours are those who are most frequently referred for professional help.
- Children showing overcontrol behaviours are often more at risk emotionally than children showing undercontrol behaviours.
- Emotional and behavioural problems among children arise primarily from what happens inside the family.
- The major cause of children's problems is how their parents relate to them.

- The most typical cause of problems arising within children themselves is low feelings about themselves.
- Children act in ways that accord with their high or low opinions of themselves.

KEY ACTIONS

- What is important for the welfare of children is that conflict between parents cease.
- If your children exhibit problematic behaviours it is important that you stay separate from these behaviours and do not get trapped into conflict.
- Do not force your way into the hidden world of your child.
- Create safety for your children to reveal their doubts and fears about themselves and you.
- Regularly check that you are interacting with your children in ways that mirror their self-worth.
- If, in spite of your best efforts, a child's problematic behaviours continue, it is then wise to seek professional help.
- The best professional help for children is either family therapy or psychotherapy; drug treatment is not recommended.

CHAPTER 8

PARENTS AS EDUCATORS

LOVING COMES BEFORE LEARNING

A repeated message throughout this book is that, unless children feel loved and accepted for themselves, they are at a serious disadvantage when it comes to educational development. Whether children who are distressed try to cope with their emotional insecurity by means of avoidance or compensation strategies, their educational development will always be a source of stress for them and they certainly will not be able to maximise their limitless capability for learning. For such children, too much energy and concentration are absorbed by their unresolved emotional conflicts.

The resolution of self-esteem difficulties and of the inner conflicts that lead to those difficulties is the first essential step in creating a positive environment in the home for a child's educational development. Without this environment, all the other recommendations in this chapter regarding parents as educators will be of little use.

In order to create a loving and supportive environment for children's education and development, parents need to:

- Avoid couple conflict in front of children
- Develop a harmonious couple relationship
- Realise their own self-worth
- Mirror the self-worth of each child
- Resolve each child's inner conflicts

- □ Be predictable, consistent and fair in the management of their own and their children's behaviour
- □ Show enduring, unconditional love and acceptance of children
- □ Engage in direct and clear communication
- □ Display regular affirmation between parent and parent, and parent and children
- □ Always keep person and behaviour separate

KNOWLEDGE IS NOT AN INDEX OF INTELLIGENCE

There is an old controversy in psychology as to whether intelligence is genetically or environmentally determined. Many children, on the basis of extremely dubious genetic evidence, have been labelled as 'stupid', 'dull', 'slow', 'average', 'above average', 'bright', 'very bright', 'clever', 'very clever', 'genius' or 'gifted'. The basis for such judgments is the level of knowledge or skills a child possesses at any one point in time. Examinations, intelligence tests and teachers' subjective assessments are measures only of knowledge and of a particular area of knowledge at that; they are not measures of intelligence. Scientific evidence now suggests that human beings (where there is no brain damage) only use about 2 per cent of their brain cells. I believe human intelligence is limitless in each individual child but how, when, to what degree and to what area of knowledge or skill that capacity is applied is determined by many environmental factors. For example, only about 1 per cent of children from areas of low socio-economic status go on to third-level education. This hardly suggests that children from these areas have less intelligence than their peers from the more advantaged areas. What it does indicate is that the former group of children have less opportunities than the latter for language and scholastic development; they tend to be less motivated and to come from homes where no emphasis is placed on educational development. By the time these children come to school, their sense of their capability in the areas most valued by the larger culture is significantly less than among their peers from high socio-economic status areas. It is a very limited view of intelligence to suggest that because a child is not thriving scholastically, he has poor intelligence. The same child may baffle you with great skill on the sports field or with his dexterity in dismantling and recon-structing a mechanical object. Typically, children from the subcultural travelling community do not shine scholastically but can outwit children from the settled community in many ways and this is also a form of knowledge.

The message that children need to hear from parents is: you have limitless capacity and once you apply yourself to any area of knowledge you will learn. Few children are given this message. Unfortunately, from very early on in their lives children tend to get labelled. All the evidence now indicates that children and adults live up or down to the labels they are given so that children (or adults) who believe, for example, that they are 'brilliant at mathematics' or 'poor readers' or 'bad at art' act in accordance with these expectations.

Language development is an essential basis for scholastic attainment. In lower socio-economic status homes there tend to be poor language skills and little verbal, visual, tactile, olfactory and auditory stimulation. Children are rarely spoken to by adults on a face-to-face basis and 'linguistic chaos' (where all speak at once) is common in these families. By contrast, in higher socio-economic status homes there tend to be high-quality verbal skills, frequent adult-to-child verbal interactions, a more stimulating environment and a richness and variety of activities.

The quality of parent–child interactions and the range of experiences available to children are the early keys to scholastic development.

Children reared in isolated or poor settings and who suffer sensory privation will be impeded in their scholastic development. It is not the amount of stimulation that counts but the quality, meaningfulness and range of experiences available.

Among children from lower socio-economic backgrounds, some of the more typical blocks to realisation of their limitless capacity in terms of educational development include:

□ Critical or dismissive parental attitudes to learning
□ Poor or no modelling of a love of and application to learning by parents
□ Poor material circumstances leading to a home environment of limited sensory stimulation
□ Restricted use of activities that promote scholastic development (for example, reading to the child, educational toys, educational games)
□ Poverty
□ Overcrowding
□ Lack of educational facilities

Some typical blocks to the educational development of children from higher socio-economic homes include:

□ Dependence on educational achievement for self-esteem
□ Overemphasis on educational achievement and overambition
□ Punishment and criticism of mistakes and failures
□ Labelling of children as 'lazy', 'stupid', 'dull'
□ Unrealistic scholastic expectations of children
□ Emphasis on scholastic performance rather than effort
□ Comparison of children with other children
□ Confusion of knowledge attainment with intellectual capability
□ Failure to distinguish between educational behaviour and the child's person

If there is marital conflict and emotional neglect within the family, then these experiences greatly affect children's educational development. All the evidence is that it is the environment of the family and the home that largely determines children's scholastic attainment.

MAKING LEARNING POSITIVE

Learning requires only positive associations if children are to retain their natural curiosity and desire to know more about the world in which they live. In looking back on school days, many people recall punishing associations with learning: criticism, sarcasm, corporal punishment, ridicule, scoldings, threats and so on. It is no wonder that many of us could not wait to get out of school. Unfortunately, the situation at home was very often similar to that in school, with either parents showing no interest or homework times becoming a time of much conflict between the parents and the children.

The first requirement for making learning positive is an absence of ridicule, scolding, corporal punishment, sarcasm, criticism, cynicism and comparisons with others – absence of anything that lessens children's belief in themselves or creates distance in the relationship with parents. The second requirement is the presence of love, encouragement, praise, affirmation, belief in the child's capacity, fun, positive firmness – presence of behaviours that increase children's belief in themselves and foster a close relationship with parents.

The behaviour and characteristics of parents who make learning a positive and challenging experience for their children are listed below. They can be usefully categorised under three main headings:

- essential parenting skills
- parents as models for learning
- basic teaching skills.

Essential parenting skills

The following parenting skills – most of which have been discussed in detail in earlier chapters – create the kind of positive emotional environment in which children can thrive educationally and in other aspects of their lives.

☐ Have an unconditional, loving relationship with your children
☐ Talk on a one-to-one basis with your children
☐ Make requests rather than commands
☐ Listen to your children
☐ See the relationship with children as always primary
☐ Do not get trapped into conflict with your children
☐ Apologise when wrong
☐ Admit your own mistakes, failures and limitations
☐ Recognise the influence of self-esteem on learning
☐ Keep your own identity issues separate from your children's educational development

The need for parents to be aware of their own protectors is important as too often adults take out their own frustrations on children. Being aware of your particular protectors (for example, quick temper, impatience, perfectionism, intolerance of mistakes) is the first step to taking charge of them. The next stage is to decide on definite action to reduce and eventually eliminate these blocks to growth. If your own frustrations arise when children are involved in education or other efforts, try to own them as yours and not 'let fly' at or take it out on the children. If you do the latter, learning begins to have punishing associations for them. Adults tend not to be very good at apologising when they have misjudged or lost control with children. It provides a good model for children to see their parents admit their mistakes and apologise, and most importantly, heals any rift that may have occurred in the parent's relationship with the child.

Parents as models for learning

The following are some of the behaviours involved if you want to be a good model for learning for your children:

- ☐ Show you enjoy reading, study and doing educational courses
- ☐ Model concentration, application and commitment to tasks
- ☐ Set time aside for educational tasks
- ☐ Make lists of things to be done
- ☐ Work for a balanced lifestyle
- ☐ Do things calmly and without rushing
- ☐ Be orderly and tidy
- ☐ Cope constructively with frustration
- ☐ Share your knowledge and ambitions with your children
- ☐ Ask for help when needed

Children imitate parents because they believe that parents are always right. When parents show a love of learning, pursue courses of study themselves, set time and space aside for concentrated and focused learning, talk excitedly about what they are doing educationally to each other and to the children, and calmly approach examinations and assessments, then their children have an enormous advantage in terms of their educational development. When children begin to imitate these positive learning actions of parents it is essential that their efforts are reinforced by encouragement, praise and rewards; otherwise such efforts may extinguish.

Parents can also be good models for learning by being orderly and tidy (not perfectionist), by making lists of tasks to be done and ticking off tasks completed, and by staying calm at all times. If you become frustrated with a task, rather than banging the table, kicking the dog or shouting at the children, you can be a model for learning by letting go of that task at that point in time, doing something calming (such as having a cup of coffee, playing a favourite piece of music, going for a walk) and returning later on to the task. If you become stuck with a task, ask for help, whether from your spouse or one of your children or perhaps a colleague. Children's brains are like sponges, and, if you model effective coping strategies, they will pick them up and automatically use them later on in their own efforts to gain knowledge.

Basic teaching skills

Some basic teaching skills for parents include:

- Knowing what to teach
- Frequently reading and telling stories to your children
- Giving your children a love of learning
- Ensuring that learning has only positive associations
- Seeing effort as an attainment
- Not confusing effort with performance
- Viewing success and failure as relative terms
- Seeing mistakes and failures as opportunities for learning
- Being patient with and encouraging your children's educational efforts
- Being positively firm in the face of a child attempting to slide out of educational responsibilities
- Regularly affirming and praising your children's capabilities and educational efforts

- ☐ Showing empathic interest in your children's educational development
- ☐ Staying relaxed and calm at all times
- ☐ Setting up study areas free of distractions in the home
- ☐ Helping your children to do things for themselves
- ☐ Helping your children to be orderly and tidy
- ☐ Helping your children to cope with frustration when learning becomes difficult
- ☐ Teaching your children how to talk positively to themselves
- ☐ Teaching your children how to relax
- ☐ Showing your children how to make lists of tasks to be done
- ☐ Doing simple time-management with your children
- ☐ Teaching your children study skills
- ☐ Dealing positively with your children's homework
- ☐ Knowing your own protectors and not taking these out on your children

When it comes to parents being actively involved in their children's educational development there are two key issues:

- what to teach
- how to teach.

What to teach

Knowing what to teach children is important because the quantity and, most of all, the quality of learning experiences in the home, both in early childhood and after children begin formal schooling, have strong effects on educational progress and development. The differences between children who have had and those who have not had enriching early learning experiences are very marked in their first days of schooling.

Traditionally the three Rs (reading, writing, arithmetic) were seen as the essential basis for children's educational development and this view still largely holds. However, the concentration on these three areas has overemphasised the development of left-brain functioning and has led somewhat to the neglect of right-brain development. Recent changes in primary, secondary and tertiary curricula are demanding more skills-based knowledge, and the early focus on children's left-brain activity has given way to equal attention to right-brain activity.

In the early years, the development of left-brain functioning depends a lot on one-to-one talking between parents and children. It is important for parents to ensure that they have the children's attention when speaking to them, and a good index of this is the maintenance of eye contact. There is a whole range of educational toys available to aid the growth of children's knowledge of language, reading, writing and arithmetic. Reading stories to children is a means of education of which most parents are well aware. It is also a wonderful opportunity for deepening the emotional bonds between parents and children. Computers have become a very important teaching aid but it is wise to check out with teachers the educational value of some of the packages on the market.

Quizzes, word games, problem-solving tasks and practise in the use of money are all activities which aid the process of left-brain activation. Equipping children with a good level of general knowledge also helps.

Activities that parents could pursue with children in stimulating right-brain development include:

☐ Eye–hand coordination tasks (for example, games, sports, painting, drawing, certain domestic tasks such as cleaning, hoovering, cooking, sewing).

- ☐ Matching objects (for example, jigsaw puzzles, Lego, Meccano, certain computer games).
- ☐ Creative/divergency challenges (for example, games for the creative use of different objects, block and Lego building, free-hand painting and drawing, problem-solving).
- ☐ Observation games (for example, 'find the missing object' games, 'what's different' tests).
- ☐ Making sense out of seemingly diverse objects or situations (for example, 'what goes with what' games or 'which is the odd one out' tests, making sense of a random series of pictures or cartoon drawings).

Children who are exposed to a wide range of these activities become 'all-rounders' and fare better in formal educational settings.

How to teach

Parents may know 'what to teach' but are unlikely to be successful if they do not also know 'how to teach'. This holds true for teachers as much as parents. Most of the items listed above under basic teaching skills focus on the 'how to teach' and have already been discussed in Chapter 6 on the mirroring of the child's self-worth. The key to 'how to teach' is being aware of the influence of self-esteem on children's educational progress and ensuring that all teaching interactions with children mirror their self-worth. Another critical factor is ensuring that children experience only positive associations with learning. This involves: seeing every effort as an attainment, seeing mistakes and failures as opportunities for learning, putting the emphasis on effort and not on performance, and remaining calm and encouraging when children experience learning difficulties. At the same time, parents cannot allow children slide out of educational responsibilities but in doing so they need to avoid getting trapped into conflict with them. Maintaining empathic interest in their educational growth guarantees children's commitment to learning. Too many parents let children get on with the business of schooling and forget that children need their parents so much to notice what they do on an everyday basis. Absence of parental interest in children's learning frequently leads to apathy and loss of motivation to learn.

Fixed study areas

Setting up fixed study areas in the home is important. You need to be sure that such areas are as free of distraction as possible and are not near the television or other sources of entertainment. When studying, it is best that children are separated from each other. Be sure to visit the children during their study times and offer help, support, encouragement and 'treats'. If asked for help avoid the temptation to do things for your children; good teaching means aiding and guiding children in a step-by-step way to do things for themselves. Doing things for them deprives children of learning to do things for themselves and keeps them helpless.

Being orderly and tidy

You need to be firm with your children from an early age with regard to being orderly and tidy, as these behaviours will transfer to their school responsibilities. Do not accept sloppy or careless work from children. Let them know firmly and calmly that acceptance of such irresponsible efforts would mean not loving them and not caring for their future. After all, an acceptance of such sloppy work implies that you (as the parent) are not loving or respecting them fully or properly as a unique person with limitless potential. Furthermore, if you see your children rushing their homework, a reminder is in order that if rushing means only half-hearted efforts, the consequence is that the work will need to be redone, thereby further delaying playtime.

Being positively firm

It is important for parents not to get into arguments with their children on issues of educational or other responsibilities. Arguments only weaken the parents' position and add fuel to children's determination to slide out of responsibility. Parents need to state firmly, calmly and precisely the effort required and then move on, not waiting for the child to argue back. If the child pursues the parent saying, for example, 'I'm not doing it, I'm going out', the parent needs to stay calm, repeat the fair expectation and let the child know the consequence of not carrying out that responsibility. The parent cannot be sidetracked by responses from the child such as: 'you don't love me' or 'I hate you' or 'if my sister asked you'd let her off'. Children (like adults) will use many ploys to get their own way. Once you remain calm and steadfast, they will know that your words matter and that they cannot break down your resolve. They now have learned what the precise limits are and this, in fact, adds to their emotional security.

Coping with frustration

Parents need to help their children to cope with the frustration that can arise when things go wrong, or they have difficulty in grasping a concept. If your child is feeling frustrated, help him to let go of the task for a while, do something calming (for example, go to the kitchen and have a soft drink, do a relaxation exercise) and then complete some other learning task that has been assigned. After the latter is completed, encourage the child to return to the earlier frustrating activity and help him through the learning task. A sense of humour lightens the whole process and also keeps the child more in touch with reality. The essential learning experience for the child is to realise that tension, frustration, anxiety and temper block the learning process and it is useless to continue until he has become calm and relaxed again.

Positive self-talk

A very valuable skill to teach children from age seven upwards is positive self-talk. Show them firstly how critical self-talk leads to worry, anxiety, fear and anger, and consequently makes learning difficult. Typical examples of children's critical self-talk are:

- □ 'I'm no good at that.'
- □ 'I can't do arithmetic.'
- □ 'I hate doing my homework.'
- □ 'I'm afraid of making a mistake.'
- □ 'All the others in the class are better than me.'
- □ 'The teacher doesn't like me.'
- □ 'I'm the dumbest in the class.'

Recall that these critical self-statements are revelations of self-esteem protectors and as such immediately indicate the need for steps to be taken by parents and teachers to mirror the child's self-worth. Helping children to alter such critical self-talk includes them in the process of realising their own self-worth. Self-statements which would counter the critical self-talk illustrated in the examples above might be:

- □ 'I have the ability to learn how to do that.'
- □ 'I may be having difficulties with arithmetic but I'm determined to continue to make efforts to learn it.'
- □ 'Doing my homework can be difficult at times but I can get help to work through these difficulties.'

□ 'It is okay for me to make mistakes as I can learn from them.'
□ 'I am my own unique person and I will not compare myself with others.'
□ 'I like and accept myself.'
□ 'My difficulties in learning indicate that either I need to make a greater effort or I need some more help from the teacher.'

Positive self-talk needs to be realistic; the child accepts present limitations and difficulties but in a way that is challenging and retains love and belief in himself. It can be very useful for children doing examinations to prepare positive self-statements for different stages of the examination process:

– before the examination
– at the beginning of the examination
– during the examination
– when feeling panicky
– after the examination.

Examples of positive self-statements include:

□ 'I am determined to do my best.'
□ 'I am going to read the examination paper calmly and con-fi-dently.'
□ 'I am going to concentrate on the question I'm doing and on nothing else.'
□ 'It's okay to feel a little nervous now but I'm just going to breathe deeply, let go of the tension as I breathe out and put my focus back on just doing my best.'
□ 'It's over now, I did my best and right now I want to move on to my next planned activity – no post-mortems.'

In teaching children positive self-talk emphasise that they need to be vigilant against falling back into the habit of critical self-talk. If they notice that they are giving themselves critical self-statements, teach them to quickly shout 'stop' to themselves and change to encouraging and affirming self-talk.

Relaxation

It is a good idea for parents to learn relaxation skills and to pass these on to their children. If children see parents practising such exercises they will be more inclined to accept them. There are many forms of relaxation including yoga, transcendental meditation, progressive muscular relaxation, hypnosis, visualisation, massage, reflexology and so on. Direct exercises which can be done by oneself are the most useful as they can be employed in any tension- and anxiety-provoking situation. Relaxation is a skill and like any other skill needs practice but eventually you can relax yourself at will. There are many tapes, books and courses available on these techniques. At the end of this chapter there is a quick and a short exercise on relaxation.

List-making and time-management

If your children come in from school complaining that they have a lot to do, sit down with them, help them to draw up a list of the assigned activities and put these in order of priority. Let them experience how pleasurable it can be to tick things off the list as they have completed them. A related skill to list-making is time-management. Whole books have been written on this topic but the more simple the system the better. From an early age – particularly when children begin to make friends, play sports, take up artistic and other activities – encourage them to diary their day in terms of what time of day they are going to engage in such activities. This will help them to see that, for example, during school days when a certain part of the day is set aside for homework and study there is less time available for other activities and some of these may need to be scheduled for the weekend. In this way, children learn the value of time and of time-management. They will also be able to monitor how effectively they use their time. If you yourself model effective time-management, then teaching your children this skill will be much easier.

Study skills

A major skill that children need to be taught is how to study (see opposite). Do not assume that this skill has been taught in the classroom. Sometimes parents and children believe that once homework is completed no further studying is required. Such a view does not foster a love of learning. Studying goes beyond homework to the excitement and challenge of exploring a given subject and seeking out new areas of knowledge. It is this type of studying that maintains children's natural curiosity to learn. When parents themselves engage in this type of study and include children in looking up things with them, the chances are high that the children will repeat this love and pursuit of knowledge.

Another, more formal aspect of studying is how to retain information. There are systematic steps to learning more effectively. Simply reading material without a study system does not lead to good retention.

Homework

Homework can be a major source of conflict between parents and children. The amount of homework assigned to children needs to be carefully monitored. A general guideline is that from ages five

SUGGESTIONS FOR EFFECTIVE STUDYING

☐ Decide on length of time of study block.

☐ Study in short time-blocks of 30–40 minutes.

☐ Arrange pleasurable activity for short breaks between study blocks.

☐ Check the list of homework and study activities and put in order of priority in terms of which activities have to be done that evening. Lower priority activities can be put onto the next day's list or scheduled for the weekend.

☐ Make out a plan for the evening's study including the targets to be reached and how they are to be achieved.

☐ When beginning to study a topic, take some time to consider what has already been learned; this sets the context for the next learning effort required. If unsure of what has been previously learned, then some revision may be needed before going on to new learning.

☐ It helps the recall of what has been studied to make notes on the main points learned. These notes make revision easier later on.

☐ When questions or assignments have been completed, it helps if parents go over the material and check whether further efforts are required.

☐ Revision is essential to retaining what has been learned. Revise regularly and final revision before examinations will be much easier.

☐ It sometimes helps first to study subjects not liked and get these out of the way. Take a break if frustration sets in and move on to a more favoured subject. Come back later to the difficult subject. Do not be afraid to ask for help if needed.

☐ Ensure that place of study is warm, comfortable, well lit, airy and free from distractions.

☐ Reward studying efforts with a favoured activity at the end of the study period.

to eight years children can get a maximum of one hour's homework, from eight to fifteen years two hours is the maximum, and from fifteen to eighteen years three hours is the desirable maximum. Some children may of course dilly-dally when doing homework and then complain about the amount of time it takes. When in doubt, check with the child's teacher how long homework needs to take. Teachers need to estimate homework time according to the learning rate of the majority of the class rather than the rate of those who learn more quickly. It is very important to bear in mind that learning is not an index of capability.

It is easier on children if you set a routine, daily time for homework. Ensure that when homework is being done there are no distractions – such as the television – and children will complete it more quickly. It is best that children do homework apart from each other and there needs to be a clear rule that they do not interfere with each other during homework. If they do interrupt each other, whether by teasing, making noises or invading each other's space, then a clearly defined sanction needs to follow. When there are problems of self-esteem within families, children can be very cruel to each other, and it is important that parents do not let children get away with either physically or verbally abusing each other. A child's life can be made miserable if an older brother or sister dominates and controls. Parents are the persons in charge of the family and older siblings cannot be allowed to control younger children. When children are doing their homework, let them know that help is available and be sure to look in on them, giving words of praise and encouragement and perhaps a 'treat'. When homework is completed, it is important that one of the parents checks the child's effort, praises the attainment achieved and when necessary points out where the next effort needs to be focused.

Where there has been a genuine and sincere effort, even though the child may have got something wrong, put the emphasis on what he has attained and let the teacher shape up the next effort needed within the classroom. Do not get a child to repeat homework just because some mistake has been made. This is very punishing for children and homework now begins to have threatening associations. It is, of course, a different situation if mistakes occur because the effort made was rushed, careless and sloppy. Then, as you have seen, parents need to be positively firm. Finally, following homework, the best reward is always affirmation and praise but children may also be rewarded with a favoured activity. This practice leads to children having positive associations with homework.

In carrying out these suggestions regarding homework it is important that predictability and consistency are maintained. If parents or other child-minders cannot be patient and calm with children's homework efforts and the mistakes they make, it is best that they are not involved in helping with homework.

Where children are consistently either attempting to avoid homework or are overdiligent and even scrupulous, these need to be recognised as signs of avoidance, hostility and perfectionism and as revelations of self-esteem difficulties. Attention to the child's self-worth is then a priority.

CHILDREN WHO ARE TROUBLED WITHIN CLASSROOMS

Children's problems within classrooms

Teaching nowadays has become a much more stressful profession and many teachers are having difficulties coping not only with children's learning problems but also with behavioural, emotional and social problems. Most teachers recognise that the child who presents with problems in the classroom comes from a problematic home situation and has self-esteem protectors. Teachers are becoming more aware of the sources of children's problems, and are more constructive and caring in their responses to children who are troubled. However, these children and their teachers need the help most of all of parents.

Earlier, a distinction was made between problems of undercontrol and overcontrol of behaviour (pp. 151–60). It is difficulties of undercontrol that primarily affect classroom management. Children who manifest their inner conflicts and self-esteem difficulties through overcontrol do not interfere with classroom order and harmony, and parents are rarely consulted about these children's behaviour. Nevertheless, these children are often at greatest risk. The typical undercontrol problems that make it difficult for teachers to conduct their classes are listed below.

UNDERCONTROL OF BEHAVIOUR AMONG CHILDREN IN CLASSROOMS

Start of class

☐ Enter room noisily

☐ Bang desk on sitting down

☐ Push and shove others

☐ Avoid eye contact

☐ Do not have the materials

☐ Ignore teacher's requests needed for class

☐ Shout out to others

During class

☐ Try to be funny

☐ Turn around in class

→

- ☐ Talk in class
- ☐ Rock in chairs
- ☐ Walk around classroom
- ☐ Talk and mutter
- ☐ Distract others
- ☐ Lift desks with knees
- ☐ Start singing or humming or whistling
- ☐ Make distracting verbal or physical noises
- ☐ Constantly fidget with apparatus
- ☐ Ignore teacher's requests
- ☐ React aggressively to feedback and correction
- ☐ Do not answer questions addressed to them
- ☐ Ignore requests for responsibility on their part
- ☐ Throw paper missiles around the class
- ☐ Interfere with other children's work
- ☐ Tease and taunt other children
- ☐ Fail to hand up homework
- ☐ Refuse to do classwork
- ☐ Have temper tantrums
- ☐ Steal other children's possessions
- ☐ Make irrelevant comments
- ☐ Damage other children's property
- ☐ Abscond from classroom

End of class

- ☐ Rush out of class
- ☐ Push and shove others

□ Shout loudly

□ Make 'smart alec' remarks

□ Avoid eye contact

□ Ignore teacher's requests for orderly exit

□ Ignore teacher's requests to stay behind

Outside of class

□ Bully other children

□ Damage school property

□ Break rule of no smoking

□ Deface walls

□ Race along school corridors

□ Steal other people's belongings

□ Shout in school corridors

Causes of children's problems within classrooms

When children regularly engage in any of these difficult behaviours, it is important that parents and teachers try to trace their causes. The sources of the problematic behaviours may lie within:

– the child
– the parent and home situation
– the teacher.

Before examining these possible sources of children's problematic behaviours, another important question to ask is whether the presenting problems are new or have been persistently occurring. Where problems are persistent, this indicates serious self-esteem difficulties and problems in the home. If the behaviour has just newly arisen, the causes are more likely to be related to something that has occurred in the immediate past, such as the birth of a sibling, change of teacher, hospitalisation of a parent, or death of a parent or grandparent. When the child is given an empathic response and allowed to express feelings and needs, these difficulties will, most likely, dissolve and the child will resume educational responsibility. It is the persistently occurring troubled behaviours that are more alarming and that require more enduring positive responses from both parents and teachers.

Look to the child

Possible causes of troubled behaviour within children themselves have already been outlined (pp. 164–5). The major cause of problems arising within children is poor self-esteem, and teachers are now becoming more aware that unless attention is paid to the self-worth of the child, little academic progress will be achieved.

Look to the parents and home situation

Possible causes of children's school difficulties arising within the family have also been considered (pp. 160–64). Teachers are well aware that, unless these home conflicts are resolved, their efforts within the school will not be powerful enough to address the troubled world of the child. The more that parents and teachers work together, the greater the chances of resolving the child's problems.

Look to the teacher

Sources of children's troubled behaviours arising within the classroom likewise have been explored (pp. 165–6). Teachers need to look to their own behaviours when attempting to trace the causes of the undercontrol responses of children within their classrooms. Very often, children's disruptive responses are triggered by the teacher's behaviour and have nothing to do with the home situation. Problematic behaviours on the part of teachers are indicators of their own underlying insecurities and self-esteem difficulties. They need to take on the responsibility to change and not continue to take their problems out on children in the classroom. The more typical difficult behaviours of teachers that can lead to problematic reactions in children are listed below. When these are a regular feature within a classroom, the teacher needs to be approached to resolve the source of children's classroom problems.

TEACHERS' DIFFICULT BEHAVIOURS WITHIN CLASSROOMS

Teacher–children communication

- ☐ Shout at children
- ☐ Order, dominate and control children
- ☐ Employ cynicism and sarcasm as means of control
- ☐ Ridicule, scold, criticise children
- ☐ Label children as 'stupid', 'dull', 'weak', 'lazy', etc.
- ☐ Physically threaten children
- ☐ Push and shove children
- ☐ Are violent towards children
- ☐ Give school work or 'lines' as punishments
- ☐ Do not listen to children
- ☐ Compare one child with another
- ☐ Are judgmental
- ☐ Do not like some children
- ☐ Do not know children's first names
- ☐ Do not call children by their first names
- ☐ Are too strict

———→

- Are impatient with children who are slow in understanding a lesson
- Expect too much of children
- Do not care whether or not children work
- Do not feel any affection for children
- Punish mistakes and failures
- Do not help when the work is difficult
- Never apologise for mistakes
- Do not say 'please' and 'thank you' to children
- Are inconsistent and unpredictable in response to troublesome behaviour

Teachers' attitudes to lessons

- Waste time
- Do not make lessons interesting
- Are not prepared for lessons
- Leave class half-way through a lesson
- Pass on to next lesson without regard to children who have not mastered first lesson
- Are programme-centred rather than child-centred

Teachers' own emotional state

- Frequently irritable and moody
- Hate teaching
- Doubt own teaching competence
- Fear loss of classroom control
- Worry about how colleagues view them
- Want children to like them
- Have low self-esteem
- Fear children

Many parents have difficulties in confronting teachers on behaviours that block children's self-worth and, because of their own self-esteem difficulties, delay or never approach these teachers. Everybody loses out when issues are not confronted, most of all the child. Do not assume that the teacher is deliberately getting at children; more often than not, the threatening actions are sub-conscious and only become conscious when confronted. When confronted, the teacher has an opportunity to review her behaviour and to resolve underlying insecurities. Your own self-esteem will also become less protective if you confront the teacher on behaviour with which you are unhappy.

Confrontation is not an exercise in blaming but in caring. The approach needs to be one of concern for the child's education; what is being requested is the cooperation of the teacher. Your purpose is to reveal the issues that are troubling the child without judging or criticising the teacher, but at the same time, requesting directly and clearly that the blocking actions on the part of the teacher cease and be substituted with more self-worth mirroring interactions. Most teachers welcome the concern and cooperation of parents, and when difficult issues are sensitively approached, change will occur. There will always be the odd teacher who will respond badly to any confrontation. If, in spite of confrontation, the problematic behaviours of a teacher persist, then further action is needed. Approaching the principal of the school is the next step, and if no response is found here, you may need to remove the child from that school for the sake of his educational development. Do not let it rest there as other children are at risk from the teacher and principal who do not show openness to change. Approaching the board of management and the parents' association attached to the school, as well as the National Parents' Council, are further steps that can be taken. Silence on unprofessional behaviour among teachers (or any other professionals) can no longer hold.

Helping children who are troubled within classrooms

When learning difficulties arise because of problems of overcontrol or undercontrol of behaviour, help needs to be given at four levels:

- the behavioural level – reducing the overcontrol or undercontrol behaviours
- the self-esteem level – mirroring the child's self-worth
- the conflictual level – resolving the conflicts within the home or classroom that are causing the child to be troubled
- the learning level – helping the child to increase educational effort.

The behavioural level

Only when the causes of the problems manifested in the classroom are identified, can effective long-term strategies be employed to help children who are troubled. A joint approach, using the resources of home and school, is needed. In the immediate situation, particularly with children who are engaging in undercontrol behaviours and who are seriously disrupting learning within the classroom and order within the school, consistent and predictable responses are required from both parents and teachers. These responses need to be fair, and given in the context of a valuing relationship with the child and a sincere and genuine search for the underlying causes of the disruptive behaviours. Sanctions agreed with the child need to be applied.

The self-esteem level

Both parents and teachers need to ensure that all their actions towards children presenting problems in the classroom are unconditionally valuing and affirming so that the children's image of themselves will begin to become more positive and accepting. How to mirror the child's self-worth has been outlined in Chapter 6.

The conflictual level

At the conflictual level, parents and teachers need to take responsibility for the problems within the home or classroom that are leading to the child's protective reactions and poor self-esteem. This may mean that the parents need to resolve their own couple conflicts or their own individual self-esteem difficulties, or that they need to develop more effective parenting skills. It may also be that parents identify emotional, physical or sexual neglect in the home by some other member of the family, or by grandparents or siblings or child-minder. Whatever the source, it needs to be dealt with firmly but positively. Within the classroom, teachers may discover that their own self-esteem problems and inner conflicts, which they are unwittingly taking out on children, are the sources of conflict. Unless teachers take responsibility for their own vulnerability, problems will persist among the children within their classrooms.

The learning level

Because of all these difficulties, children may have fallen behind in educational attainment and may now need extra help to make up for lost time and opportunities. However, without attention to children's emotional welfare, efforts at increasing their motivation to learn and application to scholastic work are unlikely to be successful. It is important that teachers advise parents on how to best help their children with learning difficulties. Regular meetings are advisable so that consistency in educational content and teaching approach is developed between teacher and parents. Patience is crucial.

PARENTS AND TEACHERS

The necessity for a better relationship between parents and teachers has already been highlighted. However, many teachers feel threatened by the increasing involvement of parents in education. Some teachers dread teacher-parent meetings and see them as something to be got through rather than as a valuable source of understanding, support and help. Parents themselves can also feel threatened by such meetings or by being asked to come to the school because of their child's problematic behaviours within the classroom. Parents are also often nervous when they want to approach a teacher with worries about their child's academic progress or with complaints from their child of difficult behaviours on the part of the teacher. There are many factors that may make it difficult for parents to approach teachers:

☐ Fear of being criticised or judged
☐ Parents' own poor self-esteem
☐ Teachers who are unapproachable
☐ Not knowing the teachers
☐ Superior protective communication on the part of teachers
☐ Parent feels like a child going to see the teacher
☐ Past punishing experiences with teachers when parents themselves were students
☐ Parents feeling inferior
☐ Formality of meeting
☐ Feeling intimidated by a principal or teacher
☐ Lack of communication between school and home
☐ Off-putting attitude on the part of the principal

There are, however, requests that parents or parents' associations can make of schools to make it easier for them to approach teachers and principals:

- Teachers to be more approachable
- Teachers to introduce themselves by their first names
- Teachers to call parents by their first names
- Encouragement of parents to come and talk about their children's educational development
- Social get-togethers
- Parents to be asked for help and advice by teachers
- Parents to be invited to participate in school development projects
- Teachers to be warm and friendly and not hide behind a professional mask
- Teachers to be open about themselves
- Regular parent–teacher meetings
- Establishment of a parents' committee in the school
- Teachers to show obvious interest and care for children
- Teachers to approach parents sensitively on their children's problems within classrooms
- The creation of an effective communication system between the school and parents so that problems are 'nipped in the bud'
- Parents to be able to ring the school when they have a concern or worry
- Information sessions on school curriculum for parents
- Setting up personal development courses for parents
- Training courses for parents on helping children with homework
- Teachers to be affirming and accepting of parents

It is equally important that parents make it easy for teachers to approach them about their child's educational progress and any behavioural and emotional difficulties which arise. Parents need to see the teacher as being valuing and caring of their child and as needing their help to increase the child's coping within the school. It is best they not perceive the teacher as blaming or judging or labelling their child (unless, of course, the teacher communicates in that way). Through regular meetings, a joint approach may be developed to aid the child. It is important that both parents attend these meetings. Too often fathers slip out of this responsibility but their cooperation and involvement are required. Regular reviews and informal contact by phone, letter or quick 'drop in' need to be made available. It is important that the parents and teacher set up, in a caring way, a fair system of responsibility for the child and that the ways of relating to the child and the demands for responsible behaviour are predictably and consistently followed through in the home and in the classroom. When a child needs to go to some outside agency (clinical psychologist, educational psychologist, family therapist, social worker), this must be done in a strictly confidential way.

The involvement of parents within schools needs to be wider than simply that of problem-solving. As has been repeated many times in this book, parents are the primary educators of their children and can do much to create positive and challenging attitudes to education in the home. They can help children retain their love of learning. Courses for parents as educators need to be established within both primary and secondary schools. Parents are not necessarily experts in how they can best provide for the scholastic development of their children. Teachers can provide them with that expertise. Other courses on the emotional, social, sexual, spiritual and physical development of children need also to be made available for parents. Parenting courses, and conflict resolution and problem-solving seminars are other means for greater contact between the school and parents. Courses on stress management and effective communication are further possibilities. When both parents and teachers attend such courses together, relationships develop in a much more equal, personal and friendly manner.

What schools need to realise and parents need to assert is that parents have knowledge, skills, expertise and abilities to care, nurture and support that can add considerably to the effectiveness of schools and children's educational development.

RELAXATION EXERCISES

Quick release of tension

The following exercise is designed for quick release of tension whenever you feel anxious, panicky or uptight.

1 Let your breath go (don't breathe in first).

2 Take in a slow, gentle breath; hold it for a second.

3 Let it go, with a leisurely sigh of relief.

4 Drop your shoulders at the same time and relax your hands.

5 Make sure your teeth are not clenched together.

6 If you have to speak, speak slowly and in a lower tone of voice.

Short relaxation exercise

☐ This exercise is designed for when you have only a short time to spare for relaxation. It is useful to have a chair with arms but ideally you need to be able to relax anywhere you find yourself. Use a cushion in the small of the back if it helps. Make sure you are warm.

☐ Sit upright and well back in the chair so that your thighs and back are supported; rest your hands in the cradle position on your lap or lightly on the top of your thighs. If you wish take off your shoes, and let your feet rest on the ground (if they don't touch the floor, try and find a book or similar object to rest them on). If you want to, close your eyes.

→

▢ Begin by breathing out. Then breathe in easily, just as much as you need, now breathe out slowly with a slight sigh, like a balloon slowly deflating. Do this once more, slowly . . . breathe in . . . breathe out . . . as you breathe out, feel the tension begin to drain away. Then go back to your ordinary breathing, even, quiet, steady.

▢ Now direct your thoughts to each part of your body in turn, to the muscles and joints.

▢ Think first about your left foot. Your toes are still. Your foot feels heavy on the floor. Let your foot and toes start to feel completely relaxed.

▢ Now think about your right foot . . . toes . . . ankles . . . they are resting heavily on the floor. Let both your feet, your toes and ankles start to relax.

▢ Now think about your legs. Let your legs feel completely relaxed and heavy on the chair, let your knees roll outwards, let them relax, let them go.

▢ Think now about your back and your spine. Let the tension drain away from your back, and from your spine. Follow your breathing and each time you breathe out, relax your back and spine a little more.

▢ Let your abdominal muscles become soft and loose. There's no need to hold your stomach in tight, it rises and falls as you breathe quietly. Feel that your stomach is completely relaxed.

▢ Let go of tension in your chest. Let your breathing be slow and easy, and each time you breathe out, let it go a little more.

▢ Think now about the fingers of your left hand . . . they are curved, limp and quite still. Now the fingers on your right hand . . . relaxed . . . soft and still. Let this feeling of relaxation spread . . . up your arms . . . feel the heaviness in your arms . . . up your shoulders. Let your shoulders relax, let them drop easily . . . and

→

then let them drop even further than you thought they could. Think about your neck. Feel the tension melt away from your neck and shoulders. Each time you breathe out, relax your neck a little more.

□ Now before moving on, just check that all these parts of your body are still relaxed – your feet, legs, back and spine, stomach, hands, arms, neck and shoulders. Keep your breathing gentle and easy. Every time you breathe out, relax a little more and let all the tension ease away from your body. No tension – just enjoy this feeling of relaxation.

□ Now think about your face. Smooth out your brow, and let your forehead feel relaxed. Let your eyebrows drop gently. There is no tension around your eyes, your eyelids slightly closed, your eyes still. Let your jaw drop, teeth slightly apart as your jaw drops more and more. Feel the relief of letting go.

□ Now think about your tongue and throat. Let your tongue drop down to the bottom of your mouth and relax completely. Relax your tongue and throat. And your lips slightly parted, no pressure between them. Let all the muscles in your face unwind and let go . . . there is no tension in your face . . . just let it relax more and more.

□ Now, instead of thinking about yourself in parts, feel the all-over sensation of letting go, of quiet and of rest. Check that you are still relaxed. Stay like this for a few moments, and listen to your breathing . . . in . . . and out . . . let your body become looser, heavier, each time you breathe out.

□ Now continue for a little longer, and enjoy this time for relaxation.

□ Coming back – slowly, move your hands and your feet a little. When you are ready, open your eyes and sit quiet for a while. Stretch, if you want to, or yawn, and slowly start to move again.

KEY INSIGHTS

□ Unless children feel loved and accepted for themselves they are at a serious disadvantage when it comes to their educational development.

□ Children have limitless capability for learning.

□ Learning is not an index of intelligence.

□ It is the features of family and home that largely determine children's educational progress.

□ Learning requires only positive associations.

□ Children protectively believe that parents are always right.

□ Children's brains are like sponges and they absorb many of the appropriate and inappropriate behaviours of parents.

□ The 'what to teach' children is only successfully accomplished when parents know 'how to teach'.

□ Doing things for children disables them.

□ Studying goes beyond homework.

□ Children presenting with classroom difficulties come from problematic home situations and have self-esteem screens.

□ Children who manifest undercontrol protective behaviours within classrooms are the children about whom teachers mostly contact parents.

□ Children with overcontrol protective behaviours do not disrupt classrooms but they are often more at risk than their peers who engage in undercontrol behaviours.

□ Persistent childhood problems are more alarming than ones which are newly arisen.

□ The more parents and teachers work together, the greater the chances of resolving children's problems within classrooms.

□ Everybody loses out when problems on the part of teachers are not confronted, most of all children.

□ Confrontation is not an exercise in blaming but in caring.

- Silence on unprofessional behaviours among teachers can no longer hold.
- Without attention to children's self-esteem and inner conflicts it is unlikely that efforts to increase children's educational attainments will be successful.
- The involvement of parents within schools needs to be wider than that of problem-solving.

KEY ACTIONS

- Resolve the self-esteem protectors and inner conflicts of your children.
- Frequently affirm your children's limitless capacity.
- Do not label your children.
- Create a high-quality verbal environment for your children wherein face-to-face talking is a regular feature.
- Provide your children with good-quality, meaningful and wide-ranging stimulating experiences.
- Eliminate ridicule, scoldings, beatings, sarcasm, criticism, cynicism and comparisons with others – anything that lessens children's belief in themselves.
- Develop love, encouragement, praise, affirmation, belief in children's capabilities, fun, challenge and positive firmness – everything that mirrors children's self-worth.
- Reinforce the efforts of your children when they imitate your positive actions.
- Try not to project your own protectors and insecurities onto your children.
- Ensure that your children's every educational effort is seen as attainment.
- Let your children know that mistakes and failure are relative terms and are opportunities for learning.

- ☐ Do not allow your children to slide out of responsibility.
- ☐ Set up study areas free of distractions in the home.
- ☐ Help your children to do things for themselves.
- ☐ Teach your children to be orderly and tidy from an early age.
- ☐ Develop the ability for positive self-talk in your children.
- ☐ Show your children how to cope constructively with frustration.
- ☐ Teach your children how to relax.
- ☐ If you find it difficult to be patient with your children when doing their homework, it is best not to be involved.
- ☐ Be positively involved in your children's homework and studying activities.

INDEX